The Militiaman at home and abroad; being the history of a Militia regiment from its first training to its disembodiment; with sketches of the Ionian Islands, Malta, and Gibraltar ... With illustrations by John Leech.

Anonymous, John Leech

The Militiaman at home and abroad; being the history of a Militia regiment from its first training to its disembodiment; with sketches of the Ionian Islands, Malta, and Gibraltar ... With illustrations by John Leech.
Anonymous
British Library, Historical Print Editions
British Library
Leech, John
1857
8°.
10105.c.17.

The BiblioLife Network

This project was made possible in part by the BiblioLife Network (BLN), a project aimed at addressing some of the huge challenges facing book preservationists around the world. The BLN includes libraries, library networks, archives, subject matter experts, online communities and library service providers. We believe every book ever published should be available as a high-quality print reproduction; printed on- demand anywhere in the world. This insures the ongoing accessibility of the content and helps generate sustainable revenue for the libraries and organizations that work to preserve these important materials.

The following book is in the "public domain" and represents an authentic reproduction of the text as printed by the original publisher. While we have attempted to accurately maintain the integrity of the original work, there are sometimes problems with the original book or micro-film from which the books were digitized. This can result in minor errors in reproduction. Possible imperfections include missing and blurred pages, poor pictures, markings and other reproduction issues beyond our control. Because this work is culturally important, we have made it available as part of our commitment to protecting, preserving, and promoting the world's literature.

GUIDE TO FOLD-OUTS, MAPS and OVERSIZED IMAGES

In an online database, page images do not need to conform to the size restrictions found in a printed book. When converting these images back into a printed bound book, the page sizes are standardized in ways that maintain the detail of the original. For large images, such as fold-out maps, the original page image is split into two or more pages.

Guidelines used to determine the split of oversize pages:

• Some images are split vertically; large images require vertical and horizontal splits.
• For horizontal splits, the content is split left to right.
• For vertical splits, the content is split from top to bottom.
• For both vertical and horizontal splits, the image is processed from top left to bottom right.

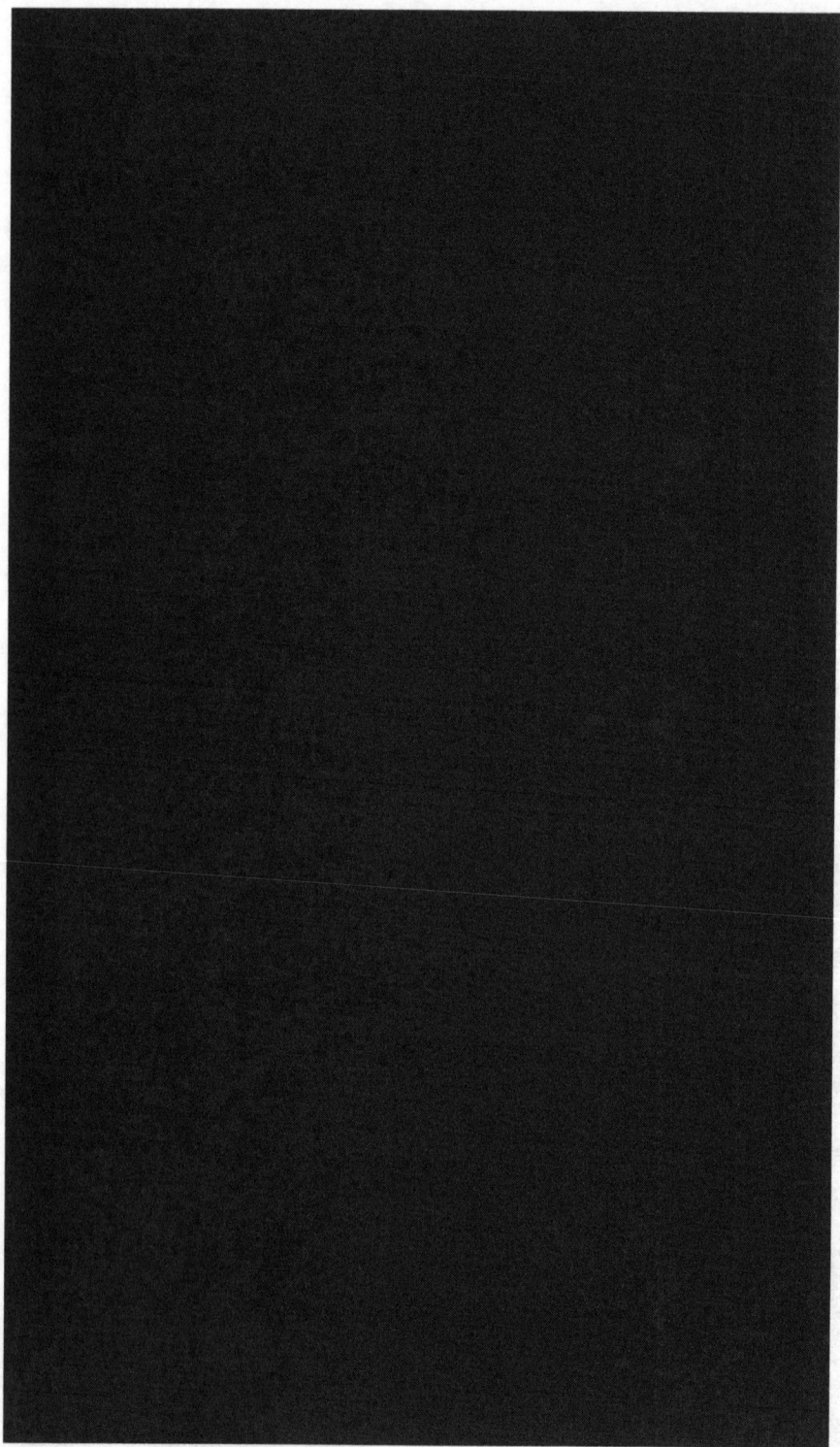

THE MILITIAMAN

T HOME AND ABROAD.

19 AU 57

THE

MILITIAMAN

AT HOME AND ABROAD;

BEING

THE HISTORY OF A MILITIA REGIMENT,

FROM ITS FIRST TRAINING TO ITS DISEMBODIMENT;

WITH

SKETCHES OF THE IONIAN ISLANDS,
MALTA, AND GIBRALTAR.

BY EMERITUS.

WITH ILLUSTRATIONS BY JOHN LEECH.

LONDON:
SMITH, ELDER, & Co., 65 CORNHILL.
1857.

EDINBURGH :

PRINTED BY OLIVER AND BOYD.

TWEEDDALE COURT.

THE MILITIAMAN.

CHAPTER I.

WHOEVER wishes to be present, in imagination at least, at the birth, parentage, and education of a militia regiment, must now step with me into the wide quiet old street of Dulminster.

Allow me to remark, *en passant*, that if the said reader be of a class to con this instructive volume on the springy cushions of a first-class carriage, or the pulpy bliss of his fireside arm-chair, I should strongly advise him never to be induced to permit a body so comfortably located to accompany the aforesaid imagination, the which, having no toes to be trod on, no nose to be frozen purple, and no ears to be deafened, will be much less inconvenienced than the said body, in standing with me shoulder to shoulder in our old-fashioned borough, whose capacious inn-yards, winding streets, and

yawning courts, serve as funnels and *culs de sac*
for the coldest winds that whistle over the coldest
downs in the West Countrie.

Permit, therefore, your imagination thus in-
voked to wander arm-in-arm with me, or ride
pick-a-back,—and welcome, if small and weakly,
—and picture to itself with me as vividly as our
duality will permit, the afore-mentioned street,
swarming with a motley group of clodhoppers
from the four corners of Blankshire.

Shepherd lads from the downs, and stout ruddy-
cheeked chawbacons from the north, with the clay
still hanging about their iron-shod lace-ups, some
of whom have trudged their thirty miles with
nought of victual to support the inner man but
raw carrots—a bad stratum for Dulminster beer,
which has fermented accordingly, and produced the
state called muzzy.

Here and there a collier lad from the western
border shows, ragged and grimy, and a pot-house
help or adventurous stable-boy, in dilapidated corduroys, and bit of hat in napless decadence, but
hanging knowingly on the cock to the last, saun-
ters, chewing straws, and sporting a top-sawyer air
of devil-may-care.

At the door of the Chequers, the centre of a group
of eager listeners, struts an old soldier, upright and
red-nosed, and full of importance, eager to exchange

knowledge for beer, and pushing the trade vigorously while it lasts. "He an old linesman as was going to show these young 'lishey officers what soldiering meant," himself conveniently oblivious of having been discharged from Her Majesty's 101st regiment as an unpromising cross between a rogue and a fool.

Bouquets of fair heads curled and ribboned, the *élite* of the shopocracy of the market-street, crane from the upper windows; their bright eyes, now glancing on the motley multitude, and now fascinated by the lieutenant-colonel's four-in-hand as it cuts scientifically out and in, and meanders gracefully round the market-cross.

Now let us proceed to set this congress of individuals into motion, and set to work in due order with the business of the day, which commenced with an attempt at a muster, the roll-call ending in a cat-call, and then no end of wheezing and bustling on the part of a squad of rather ancient serjeants, and a partial success in enforcing a division into companies according to the scale of height taken at the enlistment of each recruit. So the day wore on, and sometimes the confusion waxed greater and sometimes less, and surged into the beer-shops, and forth again to the market-place, in which, by a wide stretch of the imagination, the men were presumed to have "fallen in."

So ended a toilsome day's work, and the men were dismissed to their billets, which they tumbled into in a Noah's ark kind of fashion, dreaming, happy beasts! of a three weeks' spree, and awaiting with pleased excitement the martial wonders of the morrow.

The officers meanwhile retiring within the penetralia of the Golden Lion, discussed with some anxiety the events of the past twelve hours. Little room was there for difference of opinion. At the head of the table sat the lieutenant-colonel. His word was the fiat out and out, Mede and Persian, as it ought to be. He well knew what to do, and how to order it to be done. Few and short were his words, but they were all to the purpose, and all obeyed them, and they soon became facts, and pretty strong ones too. Work was the watchword. "A famous raw material in our hands, and twenty-eight days to cook it in. By Mars! it shall be done. To-morrow, gentlemen, at nine, we meet in the drill-ground."

CHAPTER II.

VERY chill and miserable looked the little back bed-room of the Golden Lion, lit by the dull rays of a January sun. Very cold was the first plunge from the snug blankets into the freezing vacuity. Where was the warm dressing-room, the tepid bath, the welcoming fire? Alas! we are campaigning now ; and so much for groan No. 1.

Now for the hurried shave, the pint of lukewarm water, and a dash down to the homely parlour, dignified by the title of mess-room.

Here my feelings experienced a sudden thaw. At one end was a blazing fire, the centre being occupied by a long table groaning under the savoury burden of an English breakfast. The greater number of the seats were already filled by old familiar faces, set off by the neat and soldierlike uniform of the Royal Blanks. The lieutenant-colonel, with his usual despatch, had finished his meal, and was off to the orderly-room; and the chair was filled by the tall erect figure of the senior major, his undress frock buttoned to the chin, and a medal and bars displayed on his breast, telling of many a well-foughten field in the old days of the Peninsular war. Long years ago he had left the broad lands and halls of an ancient line to prove the hereditary mettle of his blood, and now a veteran, with an eye as bright and a frame as hardy as when he clomb the mountains of Spain to do battle above the clouds, he had again left his hearth and the well-earned comforts so dear to the decline of life, to give his aid in the herculean task of moulding a new regiment, and his invaluable example as a model for the yet uninstructed youths about to assume the sword for the first time in the ranks of the Royal Blanks.

Near him was seated the junior major. He had neither the age nor the marked military bearing of his senior, but English Country Gentleman was inscribed in every line of his visage, and a cool and quiet determination of manner denoting the ability to do and dare in any position he might be placed in, stamped him with an intrinsic value truly his own; the *beau ideal* of that link between the soldier and the squire, without which the militia service would be null and void, a pageant, or a tool of despotism. It is true, that had the great Napoleon inveigled our major into the plains of Nancy, he would probably in the end have out-manœuvred him, to the serious discomfiture of the Royal Blanks, but give the major the said Nap in a narrow lane or the rick - barken of Milton Grange, and the Frenchman would have wished himself at Elba or anywhere rather than opposite such a stalwart Briton so near to his *aris et focis.*

About fifteen more officers, varying in age from eighteen to eight-and-thirty, were ranged round the table, some discussing their morning meal, and others toying with a cigar or glancing over the pages of the county paper, or looking out into the market-place, where a large concourse of our future rank-and-file were already assembled.

The greater part of the officers were composed of the neighbouring squirearchy, together with the cadets of the county aristocracy. Among them were not a few who had already drawn their swords in Her Majesty's regiments, and now stood grouped together by the attraction of old comradeship. I soon joined their conversation, which turned naturally on the work before us; and as we had all of us been taught to consider a period of six months the minimum in which a recruit could be converted into a soldier, the idea of cooking our present batch of raw lobsters in twenty-eight days seemed rather hopeless. Our speculations, right or wrong, were soon interrupted by a summons to the drill-ground, a field of some twelve acres, hired by Her Gracious Majesty from a butcher, and situated only a few hundred yards from the market-place.

Our difficulties commenced in our first attempt to move this nondescript multitude from the market-place and friendly portals of the beer-shops to the field of Mars. The first effort was made by a superannuated bugler of the Royal Blanks of other days, who extracted from a very rickety instrument a complicated burst of sounds, at once so ludicrous and diabolical, as to suggest the idea that some unlucky donkey had been interrupted in one of his most successful brays by a violent fit of sneezing. The infliction was, however, fortunately cut short by a rush of astonished rustics, which carried the musician off his legs. Not more effectual was the attempt to beat something martial out of the skin of a mouldy drum. The application much resembled the first venture of a raw footman at a double knock. It had, however, the effect of rescuing the bugler, and the drummer went down instead. Peace to the manes of these worthies. They will never figure again in the chronicles of the Royal Blanks.

At length, by the active exertion of lungs and legs, and the force of example, the seven hundred and fifty recruits who had answered to the roll were assembled in the field of their future labours. Two hours sufficed to distribute them into companies, and to hand them over to their respective captains. To each company was also allotted a pay-sergeant lately appointed from a regiment of the line. The men were hearty and full of zeal, and seconded with right good-will the efforts of the officers to get things into order. To be sure there was here and there a little grumbling. Dick wanted "to bide wi' Harry," and couldn't "stomach being alongside o' Jack," in regard to an animosity of long standing against the said Jack, in reference to an affair of poaching, followed by peaching :

Then the light company were indignant at being placed, as they imagined, at the rear of all, and commenced slipping off one by one to other companies on the sly. However great had been the difficulty of collecting them on the ground, none whatever existed in clearing it. A hint about billets and dinner was quite enough, and in a marvellously short space of time the field was deserted.

At this juncture we received a most welcome addition to our means of action, by the arrival of a detachment of non-commissioned officers and privates of Her Majesty's Thirty-eighth Regiment, and a smarter, cleaner, or more admirably appointed set of men never left a barrack-yard, and most ably and considerately did they set about

their laborious and tiresome occupation. At two
o'clock we were all again in the field. The companies were broken into squads, and the old mill
began to work again in earnest, the old clapper
spinning merrily to the same old tune—"Eyes
right; eyes left; as you was; why don't you stop
when I cries halt,"—and a Babel of the like orders
and recommendations.

In the meantime, the orderly officer had no
sinecure in his task of superintending and enforcing
regularity in the interior economy and victualling
department: At the earliest dawn, while the frost
lay on the deserted streets, and not a shop-boy had
crawled shivering from his crib below the counter,
it was his duty to trudge, wrapped in his thick
cloak, to the market-place, where the orderly men
of the different companies had been already " fallen in" by the orderly sergeant, carrying in their
hands sundry tin bowls, baskets, and buckets, and
were forthwith marched off, or, more properly speaking, followed the officer in a somewhat helter-skelter
manner to the butcher's shop. The jolly butcher,
surrounded by a gang of assistants, was all shiny
with excitement, and around him lay an infinity of
joints and slices, each labelled with a scrap of
paper fixed on it with a skewer. Then arose the
imposing voice of the quartermaster-sergeant, and
at the words, " Blue Boar, 17¾ lbs.—where's that

there Blue Boar?" the butcher repeating, "Here, Blue Boar, 17¾ lbs.," the orderly man of the squad billeted beneath the shadow of that heraldic beast, would flounder into the shop, and producing his tin, receive his allotted share, eyeing it "with stern regard of joy," and be succeeded in turn by the Golden Lion, the Black Swan, the Elm Tree, the Lamb, and the Flitch of Bacon. At times, to be sure, things did not go exactly smooth. The Lamb would not seldom get the Lion's share, and the Blue Boar involve himself in a serious wrangle with the Flitch of Bacon.

Then at dinner-time came the task of visiting these fair abodes; and, as a general rule, the hungry expectants would be found crowding the door of the dining-room, judiciously locked while the viands were in course of division. Then they would enter with a rush, and the tables would occasionally be turned, and the spread exhibited below the board instead of on it; but, by a little tact and firmness, affairs soon began to assume a more regular appearance.

You must not suppose that our embryo regiment is as yet shining in all the gay panoply of war. The machine is quite in the rough, and Government is chary in serving us out with the paint and varnish. Not a coat, or a boot, or a pot of blacking, have as yet found their way into the stores of the Royal Blanks. The costumes at present, if not altogether tasteful and appropriate, are, to say the least, various and expressive. My right hand man, for instance, assumes, for lack of helm and feather, a green and rather mutilated "Jim Crow," encircled with a yellow riband. A very extensive shirt collar shoots upward from a red bandana, and an old gamekeeper's coat, buttoned close, almost conceals a buff plush waistcoat. Stout corduroy knee-breeches, with worsted stockings of different shades of grey, encase his lower man, which is terminated by a new pair of " lace-up's," with as much iron on them as would serve to shoe a drayhorse. He looks with evident contempt on his left hand comrade, whose restless toes have worked a passage through his shoes. He is a lathy gipsy-looking lad, his fustian trousers stained with coaldust, half concealed by a dilapidated blue smock, with nothing particular under it; and he also sports a " Jim Crow," but without the riband. Next comes an unmistakable young navvy, " stained with the variation of each soil."

I will not be so superfluous as to go further down the ranks for more minute description. The larger portion of my company consists of fine grown strapping country lads, in the usual dress of a Blankshire peasant, with cheery, honest faces, and a manifest anxiety to do their best. Here is the raw material of as fine a regiment as Her Majesty, or any other potentate, need sigh for—the First Frederic of Prussia not excepted.

Let us pause here, then, for a moment, wrapt in satisfactory contemplation, and set to work resolutely to the task of training in the next chapter.

CHAPTER III.

I DO not ask the reader's imagination to keep pace
with me through the day by day moil and toil of a
three weeks' training; it would be too cruel a
handling of it; but let him suppose the training
over, and the men dispersed, and set himself by
me in the halls of my ancestors, while, in elbow
chair, before a blazing fire, with a flask of sherris,
from number one bin, I review the memories of the
past.   But I must have no questions asked, for I
have no voice to answer with, nor have any others
of my gallant corps.   I could shriek out a word of
command, in a way of my own, but as for my pri-
vate-life voice, the last I heard of it was at the
Golden Lion, just before the fogs came on.

Snow, hail, rain, and wind, have been keeping
every sensible man on his hearth-rug since my departure; and the borough of Dulminster being
about ten degrees colder than any other spot in the

county, let the cozy stay-at-home multiply the out-side miseries by ten, and find ours.

Don't fancy that we have looked at them through the window. Neither hail, rain, nor snow, has kept man or officer from the drill-ground, and the result has beat anything we could have dreamed of. Our fight with the elements and rudiments closed in triumph; for the general of the district, a veteran who knows, perhaps, more of what a soldier ought to be than any other man in England, came over and inspected us, and told us he never would have believed what he had heard of our progress, if he had not seen it with his own eyes. Now, the general is known to be no humbug, and we feel that he meant what he said.

The ground, on the day of review, was covered with snow, but the men were as steady as rocks, and in their formations of four deep deployed from column into line, and formed square from quarter-distance column, with a steadiness scarcely ex-ceeded by regiments of the line. Unremitting and arduous was our preparatory work, but the conduct of the men was beyond praise; and whether under drill, or in their quarters, they evinced a good feel-ing and spirit of discipline, that must have put to the blush those who predicted nothing but scenes of vice and drunkenness. It is but fair to assert here, and in doing so I am but speaking the bare truth, that from the energy and example of the lieutenant-colonel did all that was so creditable to the regiment take its rise. No roystering or extravagance disgraced the quiet and gentlemanly gathering at the Golden Lion. The word, and the minute, were as punctually obeyed by every individual among the officers as by the humblest Hodge in the ranks.

In the drill-ground, firmness and determination achieved their sure success; and not an oath or foul expression was permitted to the humblest of the drills. On Sunday, the men were marched to the respective churches, and their behaviour there was satisfactory to the most strait-laced frequenter of them. The inhabitants of the town, headed by the clergy, had laudably done their best to second the exertions of the officers, and established evening schools, lectures on amusing subjects, and amateur concerts, of which the men gladly availed themselves. When, at length, the day of parting arrived, the men, bounty in pocket, went soberly out of town, cheering good-humouredly, and looking forward to our next merry meeting.

The dull routine of the day's work was, of course, frequently enlivened by amusing traits of character, and odds and ends of fun and humour. The first attempts of a bumpkin to emulate the carriage and bearing of a soldier, are of themselves sufficiently grotesque. My worthy right hand man, at the word "march," persisted in violently jerking up his right leg to a right angle with his body, his foot straightened upwards till the toe pointed to his eye, and his hands convulsively clutching the seams of his trousers, his visage, at the same time, assuming a pompous gravity, only to be equalled by a College Don. The whole attitude would have made the fortune of a Grimaldi. Another would work at it like a slave, if he could only contrive to scratch his head about once in three minutes; while a third did marvels as long as he was allowed to hold a straw in his mouth, but became quite bewildered when it was abstracted. It was the hair-cutting that gave the greatest offence. To wear the hair short was to look like a jail-bird; and many heads would have preferred parting with their brains, rather than the unkempt but cherished locks that formed their ornament and pride.

Nor were the painful mysteries of drill and goose-step confined to the privates alone. A squad of officers emulated the humbler recruits, and crushed the crisp frost, and dinted the muddy sward with equal energy. Among them the Sheriff-elect, undazzled with visions of carriages-and-four, sported more mud on his regulation Wellingtons than he usually brought home on his tops from a run in the clay country.

B

By slow degrees, before the training closed, did
the Government dole out to us the requisites to
make up an uniform; and never till the men were
fully equipped in shell jacket, military trousers,
and forage cap, did we clearly see how much remained to be done, and how little relation mere
uniform bears to the gait and appearance of a soldier. One of the most striking characteristics of
the training was the almost complete absence of
crime; and most fortunate was it that it so happened, for our means of punishment were most de-
fective, and we were obliged to select non-commissioned officers at a venture from among the most
respectable-looking of the men, without previous
acquaintance with them; they were, of course, quite
ignorant of their duties, but were, nevertheless, expected to control men as ignorant as themselves of
the first principles of discipline. Of these, several
were afterwards attached to regiments of the line,
for the purpose of instruction for their future profession.

The scene that the yard of the Golden Lion presented on the morning of the fourteenth of February was not without interest and amusement.
Standing in companies at quarter-distance, each
man, as his turn arrived, marched into the store in
scarlet and blue, and then and there, in a few
minutes, emerged clad in his native habiliments,

to be received with a shout of merriment proportionate to his greater or less change of appearance; and in a few hours the men had received their arrears of pay, and the roads diverging from Dulminster were covered by a string of hearty fellows, each with a bundle suspended over his shoulder by a thick stick, and whistling and joking as he trudged along.

CHAPTER IV.

ON the fourth of April 1854, the regiment again
assembled for twenty-eight days' permanent duty,
and we were glad to find that an additional force
of sergeants from regiments of the line had succeeded such as in the former training were obviously
only efficient for the pension list, which distinguished roll they were by no means unwilling to
adorn.

We had now, in some respects, double work—
that is to say, our numbers were almost as many
again, the regiment having been recruited up to its
full complement of 1166 men, and we had 1111
actually under arms.   When I say " under arms,"
I speak advisedly, for on the thirteenth of this
month the Royal Blanks had the honour of carrying the Queen's musket for the first time in her
service.   Thanks to the solid foundation which had
been laid at the last training, our personal labour

had become proportionally light, and the progress of the men was as satisfactory as ever; and on the twenty-second, just nine days after the first musket had been served out, the first levy went through the manual exercise as a regiment in line in a most creditable manner. The lieutenant-colonel was, as usual, never absent an instant from his post, but might be seen everywhere directing and advising; and the colonel, who took equal interest in the success of the regiment, inspected our progress frequently, and encouraged both men and officers by his presence among us, and the energy with which he brought his well-earned personal influence to bear in causing the regiment to be provided with all necessary stores and material, and in making their conduct and exertions to be known and appreciated in the highest quarters.

During the progress of the training we spared no exertion to promote the comfort and amusement of the men; and on the twentieth, finding that the annual fair and cattle-market would fill the old town of Dulminster with traders and tipplers, we marched the regiment to the top of Breezy Hill, and on the beautiful down-lands in its rear we spent a merry day in getting up a variety of athletic games, races, and leaping-matches. The majority of the prizes were won by a little stumpy fellow, who answered to the euphonious name of Ginger, who, totally unknown when he ascended the hill, descended it a hero, and from that moment became a man of mark in the Royal Blanks.

On the twenty-eighth, our exertions came to a close, and we were highly complimented by the gallant colonel who had been deputed to inspect us, and the afternoon was occupied in returning our arms and accoutrements into store. We had contrived to vary the monotony of our leisure hours by the old military resource of private theatricals. Our stage and properties were on a limited scale; but as genius aroused overcomes the drawbacks of situation, and none but friends were present, our exertions met with most entire success, and we received the plaudits of a discerning public in the shape of about fifteen of our own comrades.

We were just on the point of departing for our homes when we suddenly received an order to remain out for a period of fifty-six days; but Parliament, in its wisdom, discovered that such an order being illegal it had better be rescinded, so a counter order set us at liberty, and on the first of May the men returned home. Thus ended the last of the preliminary trainings, for on the tenth of June following, a day ever to be remembered in the chronicles of the Royal Blanks, the regiment at length assembled for permanent embodiment, until

such time as Her Majesty should find herself in a
position to dispense with their services. Before
the close of the day about 900 men had answered
to the roll-call. Of the absentees many had en-
listed in the line, and several of the finest men in
my company were now in the ranks of the Guards,
Artillery, and Marines. We had no reason, however, to complain of those that remained to us, and
after distributing the arms and accoutrements, and
mustering the men on parade, we set seriously to
work at the very important task of selecting the
men for permanent embodiment, and sending back
to their homes on leave of absence such as could
best be spared, who were nevertheless under warning that their services might be required in future,
and that they were bound to hold themselves in
readiness to rejoin the regiment whenever they
received the proper notice. In the process of selection, we did our best to reconcile the requirements
of the service with the peculiar circumstances of
each respective man. First of all, we sent home
such as had large families dependant on them, then
exceptional cases, such as the only son of a widow,
or the sole bread-provider of a sick household.
The men behaved very well, and submitted cheer-
fully to our decisions; but the anxious mute appeal
of their countenances, when some of these cases
were under consideration, was hard to withstand,

and proved to us beyond a doubt that the hearts of the poor are in their right places.

The companies were at length selected under the eye of the lieutenant-colonel, and drawn up under the shelter of the long market-house: the rain pattered on the roof, and the cold blasts swept through it, imparting an additional chill to its dank wet pavement—a veritable English June day. On the outside, or within their billets, stick in hand, and with their bundles ready fastened, were the enfranchised members of the corps, ready to bid a hearty good-bye, or to exchange a little good-humoured chaff with their comrades in the ranks. In the evening the weather admitted of a parade in the old drill-ground, the cradle of the Royal Blanks, so soon to be exchanged for a more extensive field of enterprise. Next day, being Sunday, we attended divine service in the fine old church of St Mary, and had an excellent bit of good advice from the worthy vicar. On Monday, the business of selecting the service companies being finally arranged, the men were paraded, and the captains addressed a few words of encouragement to their respective companies, which were received with hearty cheers.

We now set to work to put in order the internal economy of the regiment, and transact a multitude of minor affairs not interesting to the public in general, but indispensable to the efficiency of a corps daily expecting the route for distant quarters.

At earliest dawn on the morning of the sixteenth of June, the regiment, consisting of sixteen officers, twenty-six sergeants, ten drummers, and six hundred and two privates, mustered for the last time in the market-place, and the slumbers of the drowsy citizens were broken by the larum of bugle and drum. The new colours, the gift of the colonel, had arrived just in time, and were unfolded in their pristine glory, and the ensigns held gallantly on to them, undismayed by the untried perils and fatigues of a twenty-four mile's march. The day was of the kind called muggy, with a soft misty rain, and as the men marched cheerily along the broad highway, with its fringe of noble elms, the absence of dust and knapsacks, the two great drawbacks of a military promenade, and a song or two from the gifted few learned in ballad lore, and endowed with lungs to match, made the toil light; but welcome rose the breezy uplands as we breasted them, and we breathed freer as we gazed over their pathless expanse of down, unbroken by mound and hedge, and unscarred by the furrow. Then came the halt with gibe and jest, and judicious allowance of beer, that carried us along merrily with many a cheer and chorus, till the tall spire of our famous old cathedral hove in sight, and proclaimed to us that our day's work drew towards a close, and at length under its shadow we came to a welcome halt. Then billets were distributed, and anon the quiet old streets were speckled red, and the kitchen fires of the humbler hostels irradiated an unwonted circle in martial attire, and flashed on brass and steel.

Next morning the men mustered, regular and sober, and ensconced snugly in railway cars, were whirled in a few minutes beyond the confines of their native county, and before noon, the tall leviathans of Her Majesty's fleet were visible, rearing their mighty masts above the waters of their harbour home. The grandeur and novelty of the view filled the men with excitement and delight, and all were in high good-humour as they leaped briskly from the cars, and were *en route* without loss of time for their allotted destination in the Anglesea and Fort Monckton Barracks, which they reached after a mile's march, and halted in the square where they were told off to their respective quarters.

CHAPTER V.

THE scene now rises on the heathy outskirts of that little town, alike notorious and amphibious, on whose walls hangs the fig so rare of ripeness on English soil. In whose streets abound soldier, sailor, and marine, strutting or rolling, from morn to dewy eve, and sometimes later, hand in hand, or fist to fist, as love or strife, beer or bile, may be ascendant over the passing hour. Where Queen's biscuit has its birth, and salt junk its abiding-place, ere they start in company in bag or barrel to the four quarters of the globe. In Gosport in fact, and scarce beyond the shadow of that vast hospital where Britannia acts the Miss Nightingale to her sick and wounded tars, with a wild heath in our front and our barrack-homes in our rear, we were unceasingly employed in licking into regimental shape the willing but as yet uncouth materials that composed the Royal Blanks. We soon contrived, by the assistance of a smart drum-major, to disturb the neighbourhood every night by rattling off a very respectable tattoo, and worked away at guards and sentries till the men roared like furies at anybody who passed within a quarter of a mile of them, and would have impounded the Lord Mayor if he had chanced to come within their reach after hours. While a portion of the regiment were hard at work at the battalion movements in the wide common that stretched towards the villas of Anglesea, a party under the superintendance of some of the smartest of the non-commissioned officers were going through the mysteries of relieving guard in sly corners, and keeping watch and ward over imaginary strongholds supposed to contain national treasures of unspeakable value. The whole art of cleaning and arranging barrack-rooms, and the subtleties of converting ration-beef into good soup, were also in course of inculcation. The young non-commissioned officers soon began to be polished up to the knowledge of their important duties; so that Dick Watts, late of Fiddler's Green, began to esteem himself a very different person as Corporal Richard Watts of the Royal Blanks light bobs. The march to church was above a mile, and, by help of drum and fife, an improvement became, week by week, evident in our general steadiness and ability to keep step well together for long distances. In their hours of leisure the men amused themselves with athletic games, or exercised themselves in attaining the noble art of swimming on the fine beach, over which the waves broke fresh and clear, till they fell in foam against the sea-wall that protected the barracks.

Passing events now began to indicate that our services would be shortly required for the purpose of relieving a portion of Her Majesty's troops destined for active service in the Crimea; and the order at length arrived; and on Friday the 14th of July, a day memorable in the annals of the Royal Blanks, at nine o'clock in the morning, after a hard set-to at brushing the barrack-rooms into order and despatching breakfast, the regiment marched, with drums beating and colours flying, and by eleven had passed over the harbour-mouth on the floating bridge, marched up the High Street of Portsmouth mid the curious glances of the spectators, and taken possession of the Clarence Barracks, just vacated by a battalion of the Rifles; and in less than an hour a party, consisting of one captain, two subalterns, three serjeants, four corporals, one drummer, and a hundred and thirty rank-and-file, proceeded to the dockyard, and, relieving the men of the Thirty-fourth Regiment, had the honour of mounting guard over the most important station in Her Majesty's dominions. I only do the men com-

mon justice in saying, that, as far as essentials are
concerned, we had reason to be proud of the manner in which they went through the ceremony, and
the creditable appearance which they presented
individually. We had not yet sported knapsacks,
and the haversacks which did duty in their stead
were certainly more useful than ornamental; but
our arms were bright, and our forage-caps—for the
authorities had not yet favoured us with chacos—
were cocked in the most knowing and defiant manner their wearers could suggest. In visiting the
round of sentries, the officer in command was accompanied by a superintendent of that most efficient body of men the dockyard police, who, in
addition to pointing out the duties required from
the respective sentries, explained the recondite dis-
tinctions of naval uniform, in order that the men
might know to whom they were expected to "carry
arms," and to whom to "present" them. Three
rings of gold lace on the sleeve betokened a captain, and entitled the wearer to a "present." This
occasioned a little confusion at first, for a tall,
severe-looking man in blue, with three light-coloured stripes on his wrist, was received with all
the honours due to the captain of a man-of-war,
though only enjoying the rank of a serjeant of police. The men turned out well both by day and
night, and received the field-officer on duty with

the customary honours without mistake or hesitation. The port-admiral paid the captain on duty the compliment of inviting him to dinner, the subalterns obtaining their humbler fare and neat wines from the well-known adjoining hostel called the Ship and Castle. The next day at eleven another party of our regiment relieved their comrades, who were marched back to their quarters. This may fairly be considered as the commencement of our career in the character of efficient soldiers. With much still to learn, and a full determination to learn it, we were yet entitled to assume that our past labours had not been in vain, and that the Royal Blanks had up to this time acquitted themselves right royally.

CHAPTER VI.

FATE, or rather the Horse Guards, had not destined us to be the sole representatives of militia chivalry in this garrison. Scarcely had we taken possession of our new quarters when a special train arrived with the Red Rose Regiment band and colours, who straightway set up an opposition establishment at the Cambridge Barracks, a distance of only a few hundred yards. Now, two cocks of such true fighting mettle as the Royal Blanks and the Red Roses could scarcely perch on a couple of dunghills in such close proximity without a little crowing and scratching of the straw, and the two soon began to look askance at one another. On the first Sunday, at the close of divine service, the two regiments were paraded for the purpose of marching off, and the regimental number of the Red Roses being higher than that of ours, they were doomed by the etiquette of the service to fall in in our rear.

This was construed into a great blow to their dignity, and seemed to cry aloud to all the gods of war for vengeance. Was not the Red Rose capital a mighty city! and who are these Blanks?—Pshaw, chawbacons! clods! bumpkins!

The shades of evening were just closing over the sultry streets of Portsmouth, and the officers of the Royal Blanks had just seated themselves round the mess-table, when a mighty shout arose, and echoed along the narrow lane that leads to the barrack-gate. Royal Blanks and Red Roses were in full conflict. The Blue emblazoned Boar, the Bear and Ragged Staff, with such mottoes as "Neat Wines and Spirits," "Double X and Old Tom," were the escutcheons under which these modern heroes picked their quarrels and fought them out. Not an atom of glass remained in the windows of the "Soldier's Repose." "The Castle" had been stormed, and in the very bowels of the "Bear" raged a hidden contest in the dark, hideous with growls and groans. To drop all metaphor: one of those disgraceful scenes, a military riot, had suddenly broken out. The mess-room was deserted in an instant. The lieutenant-colonel was first in the field, and soon played the Achilles in the battles. To a consummate power of command, and the skill and nerve to act promptly at a crisis, nature had added a giant's strength. By his energy

and decision the rising storm was crushed for that
night at least, before it had time to extend and
grow formidable.   Pickets were hastily fallen-in
and placed under the command of officers, and all
stragglers being finally collected, the barrack-gates
closed for the first time on the Royal Blanks in
disgrace, and the officers resumed their places at
table, anxious and annoyed, and presaging future
troubles.   To such as are aware of the inveteracy
with which these regimental quarrels frequently
become perpetuated between the rival corps, and
have witnessed the horrors of these impromptu
engagements, the distrust and annoyance of the
officers will need no explanation.   Imagine upwards of a thousand infuriated men, raging for
blood, they know not why! shrieking out oaths
and threats, their bayonets red with manslaughter!
all discipline cast away: brick-bats, belts, blud-
geons—any weapon that ingenuity in evil can suggest, welcome, so long as it may serve to help
destruction : all fair-play scouted, all mercy scoffed
at : the prostrate trampled on and brutally kicked :
maimed wretches carried to the hospital, not a few
never to quit it alive.   Imagine this, and know
further, that when at last the brutal riot has been
quelled, the combatants only separate to renew the
sanguinary scene at the first opportunity.   The
next day an ominous and excited appearance per-

vaded the ranks of both corps, but the command-
ing-officers had arranged their plans of action, and
prepared for the worst. As evening approached
pickets patrolled the streets, and a strong inlying
picket, commanded by a captain, was kept under
arms within the barracks. The necessity for such
precautions was soon apparent. Parties of both
regiments, with scowling looks and muttered threats,
began to form in knots at the corners of the streets,
and, joining one with another, increased gradually
to a compact mass, and moved towards the streets
in which they knew their rivals were awaiting
them. A few partial encounters had already taken
place, and the shopkeepers had begun to close their
shutters in alarm, when the pickets of both corps
advanced quietly and firmly, and succeeded in getting their comrades once more within the barrack-
gates, which were again closed for the night. Truth
has compelled me to detail this black page in the
history of our dearly-beloved regiment. Unwill-
ingly has my pen moved over the blotted page;
but I now close it for ever, and am happy to be
able to affirm with equal truth, that from this time
forward, in spite of much shrugging of shoulders
and evil prognostications on the part of the authorities, the men had the good sense to see the error
of their conduct. A mutual reconciliation took
place, and whether on service, in quarters, or in

canteen, the Red Roses and Royal Blanks became fast friends and good comrades.

On the 19th of July, we made our first essay at brigade-movements, in conjunction with our late rivals the Red Roses, the colonel of the latter corps commanding. The regiment now commenced entering upon a course of instruction in the varied duties of a soldier, far beyond anything that had been originally contemplated at the formation of the corps. The slow march was sedulously practised, and the movement by threes was used in addition to our late formation in fours. At the same time, the men began to assume individually the carriage and smartness of the soldier, and the sentries became day by day more clean and alert. In the interior economy of the regiment, and the minutiæ of barrack-rooms, some progress became apparent. The men commenced to pride themselves on the neatness with which their beds were folded, and the whiteness of the tables and forms. Many of their duties were performed in conjunction with Her Majesty's Thirty-fourth Regiment, and in that smart and highly-disciplined corps the men had before them a model worthy of imitation in every branch of military acquirement ; and the advantage they derived from it was of the highest importance. On July the 28th, the regiment was brigaded for the first time with the Thirty-fourth

and Red Roses, passed in review order before the general, and executed several manœuvres under his command. Two days afterwards the morning drill was attended by several hundreds of the friends and relatives of the men, who had arrived by a special train for the purpose of witnessing the deeds of their scarlet-clad belongings.

The old father, with his clean corduroys and home-knit worsted hose, with the wide-skirted coat of blue, spangled with gilt buttons, drawn from its snug retreat in the old cottage-chest, and carefully brushed for the holiday, escorted his "old woman," in black scuttle-shaped bonnet and broad-flowered chintz gown, the sweetheart bringing up the rear with a huge nosegay in one hand and a white handkerchief in the other, somewhat mottled with finger-marks. This novel flight of Arcadians settling unannounced on Southsea Common was quite a show for the spectators, as they ran, hobbled, laughed, and shrieked, intruding in ignorant curiosity on the space required for drill, and constrained thereby to an unwilling participation in the manœuvres of the parade. At times all became confusion : grenadiers charged their uncles and aunts, and Light Bobs skirmished with their grandmothers. By command of the lieutenant-colonel, the men were set at liberty from all drill and duty for the rest of the day ; and I am glad to have it in my power to record, that although the excursionists did not depart till a late hour, there were only three soldiers out of barracks at tattoo. The same event occurred again in August, and the result was equally satisfactory. In the meantime the county of Blankshire had not been forgetful of their military representatives, and, to testify their sense of the credit that had accrued to the county by the character the regiment had acquired, put their hands into their pockets, and presented the officers' mess with a very handsome service of plate, including an elegant and costly candelabrum, and in addition a complete set of brass instruments adapted to the requirements of a full military band. We lost no time in putting these into the hands of a select body of men, and having the good-luck to secure the services of a very able and industrious bandmaster, they soon learned the rudiments of the science, and improved so rapidly, that on the 1st of October they played the regiment to church and back in a style highly creditable to them ; and on the 7th of December, on the occasion of the colonel dining at mess after a visit of inspection, they made a very successful *début* as performers of a selection of operatic music.

On the 25th of August, we were brigaded on Southsea Common, with the Artillery, a battalion of Marines and Rifles, and two Militia regiments, in contiguous columns at quarter-distance; and at three o'clock Prince Albert, attended by a brilliant staff, arrived on the ground, and the troops passed in review before him, and then went through the evolutions of a field-day. This was the first occasion on which his Royal Highness had seen militia regiments manœuvre in brigade, and he was pleased to express his approbation, which was conveyed to us in the following regimental order :—

"REGIMENTAL ORDERS.
"*Portsmouth, August* 26.
"The lieutenant-colonel commanding has much pleasure in informing the Regiment, that Field-Marshal His Royal Highness Prince Albert expressed his high approval of its appearance and manœuvring on yesterday's field-day.

"Its appearance was highly creditable to all ranks, and the commanding-officer trusts that the gracious approval of His Royal Highness may stimulate all to renewed exertions towards improvement."

On the first of August, the men fired blank cartridge for the first time, to their great amusement, having been long anxious to make trial of their new weapons; and on the twenty-eighth, targets were erected, and the men exercised with ball at distances varying from eighty to one hundred and fifty yards. The appearance of that large tract of waste land, called Southsea Common, must at this period have gladdened the heart of any man who prided himself on the pomp and circumstance of war, and struck consternation into the deepest recesses of the breeches pocket of a follower of the school of Manchester. Scarcely grew a weed on that arid turf that was not daily trodden by the passing foot of some recruit drilling against time, and eager to be pronounced fit to join the ranks of his comrades on that distant shore, whence came day by day such startling rumours and records of spirit-stirring deeds. The firm steady tramp of the battalion; the agile tread of the rifleman; the fitful rumble of the artillery wheel; the sharp clear commands of the drills; the ringing bugle; the rattling volley, and the frequent crack of the minié, reverberated from morn to dewy eve; while the deep diapason from the heavy guns of the instruction-ships in harbour, and the bomb and rocket practice at Fort Cumberland, "joined in the dreadful revelry." If a fitful breeze eddied over its surface, it was not thistledown that it whirled aloft, but the blackened fragments of spent cartridges, and hundreds of ragged urchins grovelled gregariously, collecting metal in the shape of exploded copper caps. The health-seeking cockney, as he strutted along the sea-shore, or sunned himself on the slopes of Southsea Castle, inhaled a divided fragrance of sea-weed and gun-powder, and in his ears rattled an incessant alarum, suggesting to him the idea of confinement in a vault, with a bevy of London footmen practising double knocks on the door.

At this period an addition was made to the clothing of the regiment, which put them on an equality, in point of personal appearance, with their comrades of the line. The shell jacket, haversack, and forage cap, were superseded by a neatly fitting coatee, with good broad lace and the royal facings, a chaco with an ornamented silver plate in front, and resembling in shape that of the Royal Artil-lery, and a light, commodious knapsack, with the regimental number painted in white figures on the back. The flank companies were, at the same time, presented by the colonel with a set of wings for the shoulders, of superior manufacture, and the care the men took of them proved that they appre-ciated that distinctive ornament.

On the twenty-fifth of October, the regiment was inspected by Major-general Breton, commanding the South-western District, who was pleased to express his entire approbation of the state in which he found the regiment, and which was communi-cated to us in the following regimental order:—

" *Portsmouth, October* 26, 1854.

" The officer commanding has great pleasure in congratulating the officers, non-commissioned officers, and men of the Royal Blankshire Militia, on the result of the major-general's inspection, which was highly creditable to the regiment in every respect. The soldier-like appearance, and general steadiness of the men under arms, prove that much attention has been paid, both by officers and men, during the short time that has elapsed since the embodiment of the corps; and the commanding-officer hopes, that by a steady adherence to discipline, and good conduct, the regiment may ever deserve the good character it now has."

The rains of autumn had now begun to convert the common into a slough of despond for drill, and the evolutions of a battalion could no longer be performed on its slippery surface. Twice a-week, however, in order to accustom the men to the use of their new knapsacks, the regiment was marched out a distance of four miles or so, and the enlivening strains of their band, and an incessant series of songs, of a jovial rather than select character, and a train-attendant of nut and apple huxters, beguiled the tedium of the way, and rendered the sanitary effects of the march additionally efficacious. At this period a circumstance occurred which put to a severe trial the steadiness and discipline of the corps. Anxious to send every available man to the seat of war, the Government cast longing eyes on the tempting store of ready-made food for powder that lay packed in the ranks of the embodied regiments of militia; and an order in council was issued, empowering militiamen to enlist into the regular army; and in order to encourage the different regiments to do so to as great an extent as possible, commissions in the line as ensigns without purchase were promised to such eligible candidates as the colonel might recommend, at the rate of one commission for every seventy-five privates so recruited. To expedite the effects of this order, a troop of recruiting sergeants, representing every branch of the service, poured into the different barracks on the morning of the twenty-fourth of November, and beer and blarney reigned supreme for several days in succession. About 150 men of our regiment availed themselves of the privilege, and generally selected the ranks of the Guards and Marines, and many a fine fellow from my own company now rests below the blood-stained soil of the Crimea. In a few days the sergeants were withdrawn, and the regiments returned to their propriety.

CHAPTER VII.

THE year fifty-five closed on a most eventful epoch
in the military history of our country. Captain
Sword had commenced splitting up Captain Pen
with a vengeance. Beneath the snows of the
Crimea lay the flower of as gallant and well disciplined a host as ever left their native shores to
meet a hostile nation in arms. The desire of being
allowed to relieve our comrades of the line in garrison duty on foreign stations had long been prevalent in the ranks of the militia, and in none did
it assume a definite form earlier, or more earnestly,
than in those of the regiment whose career I am
now describing. So unanimous was this feeling
ascertained to be among many of the best disciplined regiments, that an act was passed for the
purpose of rendering such a proceeding effective;
and from the importance of the document, and the
bearing it has on the subject I am now treating, I

make no apologies for transcribing in full such extracts from its provisions as were sent down by Government for the information of the regiment.

" *War Office, January* 15, 1855.

" Sir,—In transmitting for your information the accompanying copy of the Act of Parliament authorizing Her Majesty to accept the services of the militia out of the United Kingdom, I have the honour to acquaint you that the following will be the conditions under which the voluntary offers of the militia to serve out of the United Kingdom will be accepted.

" 1*st*, Only three-fourths of the actual establishment of any regiment can be allowed to serve out of the United Kingdom.　The companies proceeding abroad will consist of ninety rank and file each, and the remainder of the regiment will form an embodied depôt at the county headquarters.

" 2*d*, The establishment of the companies proceeding abroad will consist as follows :—

1 Lieutenant-colonel ;
1 Major ;
1 Captain,　⎫
2 Subalterns,　⎬ to each company ;
　　　　　　　　⎭
1 Paymaster ;
1 Adjutant ;

1 Quartermaster ;

1 Surgeon ;

1 Assistant-surgeon ;

1 Sergeant-major ;

1 Quartermaster-sergeant ;

1 Paymaster-sergeant ;

1 Armourer-sergeant ;

1 Hospital-sergeant ;

1 Orderly-room clerk ;

5 Sergeants per company, including colour-sergeants ;

1 Drum-major ;

2 Drummers per company ;

5 Corporals per company ;

85 Privates per company.

" 3d, If the regiment is commanded by an officer of the rank of colonel in the militia, there will be objection to his proceeding with the regiment, retaining of £1, 2s. 6d. as such, but he can only rank with the officers of Her Majesty's forces as a lieutenant-colonel of militia.

" 4th, The pay and allowances of officers, non-commissioned officers, and men, will be the same as in the line, as far as they may be applicable to the militia forces. The non-effective allowance to field-officers is not admissible in militia regiments, but the 3s. a-day to the commanding-officer, and contingent allowance to the captains, at the regulation-rate, will be admitted. The mess-allowance granted to officers of embodied regiments of militia in the United Kingdom, will not be admissible at stations abroad where the allowance is not issued to line regiments.

" 5th, Clothing for the non-commissioned officers and men will be provided under the regulations already issued to embodied regiments of militia, and compensation in lieu of clothing, whenever liable to be claimed, will be allowed, under such regulations as may be fixed for the infantry of the line.

" 6th, Such militiamen as may wish to volunteer for service out of the United Kingdom will be required to make a declaration, that of their own free-will and consent they do so volunteer; and that such offer is to be purely voluntary should be particularly explained to each man, is pointed out in clause 3 of the Act, and that on their being released from their previous engagement in the militia, they will take the oath prescribed in the accompanying form, to serve for five years in the United Kingdom, Gibraltar, Malta, or the Ionian Islands.

" 7th, The following bounty will be allowed for each man who may volunteer for such extended service, and take the prescribed oath to serve out of the United Kingdom :—

£2, to the man on volunteering and taking the oath.

£1, to be laid out in providing him with extra necessaries.

£5, to be issued to him at the rate of £1 a-year, or quarterly.

———

£8, Total.

" The issue of the annual bounty will be subject to the same regulations as that granted to militia-men serving in the United Kingdom.

" I have to request, therefore, that, on the receipt of the order of the Secretary of State referred to in the first clause of the Act, you will fully explain to the non-commissioned officers and men of the regiment under your command the above-recited conditions under which they may volunteer for service out of the United Kingdom, and that you will then transmit to me a nominal list of the officers, and a certified statement of the number of men who are prepared to offer their services under the provisions of the Act, with a view to the issue of such further instructions as may be necessary for carrying the offer into effect.—I have the honour to be, &c.

" SIDNEY HERBERT."

The morning of the eighteenth of January was

the day selected for submitting the proposal of Government to the men of the regiment. Before parade, the captains of the respective companies addressed a few words to their men in explanation of the terms offered, and impressing upon them the fact, that nothing was to be done except of their own free-will and choice, and that all who had objections to go abroad would be included in a depôt to be formed before the time of embarkation, and to be quartered at Dulminster. The regiment paraded in the barrack-yard at the usual hour, and after inspection formed square, and the lieutenant-colonel, riding into the centre, addressed to them a few stirring words, full of pluck and heartiness, which roused a visible excitement in the ranks. He had no sooner concluded than the band made the old barrack-walls ring again with a burst of martial music, and the ensigns unfolded the rustling silk of the colours, emblazoned with the gallant cross of St. George, and men and officers, with one voice, startled the distant streets with a peal of hurrahs, such as the lungs of Englishmen only can give out, and Englishmen alone hear without alarm. The men were then dismissed, and hurried to the orderly-room, and, before evening, a body of men, exceeding by a considerable number the proportion required by Government, had enrolled themselves for foreign service.

D

I have, but one more incident to relate, and shall
then close the regimental annals of fifty-four. The
recruiting sergeants of the regulars had thinned our
ranks, and it became necessary to make an appeal
to the old county for a fresh supply. To facilitate
this object, as well as to give our countrymen a
taste of what we could show them in the line of the
grand and glorious, the sergeants of the regiment,
accompanied by the band and drums, took possession of a special train, on the morning of the fifth
of December, and were soon set down in the county
town of Blankshire. They were followed by the
whole of the officers, and, for that day at least, the
streets of the old city looked lively again, and recalled, to the older portion of the inhabitants, the
scenes and doings in the days of the late war. At
the close of the day, the colonel and lieutenant-
colonel entertained the officers to a gallant spread,
and all departed in high glee, by a special train, to
headquarters. The railway carriages must have
been most enjoyable next morning, so intensely
had they been smoked, and with such choice weeds.
Although the uncertain climate of our country succeeded in marring, to some extent, the pleasure of
the spectacle, by a ceaseless downfal of rain, yet
the experiment proved successful, and an officer
having remained behind with a recruiting party,
" turning the green one red," as Macbeth says,

a sufficient number of stalwart " green ones " were
to be seen in a few days performing the graceful
evolutions of incipient soldierhood in the barracks
of the Royal Blanks.

CHAPTER VIII.

HER Majesty's Government did not keep us long in suspense regarding their intentions, as may be seen by the date and contents of the following letter :—

        "*Horse Guards, 3d February* 1855.

"SIR,—The General Commanding-in-chief having received a notification that her Majesty's Government has accepted the offer of the Royal Blankshire Militia for service abroad, I am directed to signify his Lordship's desire that you will cause the regiment to be held in readiness for embarkation for the Ionian Islands, as soon as tonnage is provided.

"You will be pleased to call for, and transmit to this department, a return in duplicate of the number of officers and men who will be available for embarkation, which return is to be accompanied by a separate nominal list of officers who take their families with them, showing distinctly the number and quality of the individuals for whom accommodation will be required on board ship.

"You will be also pleased to direct the commanding-officer to make the necessary application to this department for squad bags (if not already in possession,) as well as for the due proportion of capes allowed for a regiment on embarkation, as directed by the circulars of the sixteenth of November and twenty-sixth of December last; and, before embarkation, you will be pleased to cause a minute inspection to be made of the regiment, and a report as to its state of equipment and efficiency transmitted to me for the General Commanding-in-chief's information.

"I have only further to request that you will impress on the commanding-officer the necessity of the strictest attention being paid to the regulations for troops on board ship (particularly as regards smoking between decks,) as detailed in the general orders for the army, from which no deviation is sanctioned, except in respect to the number of women to accompany the regiment, the Secretary-at-war having consented, in the case of the militia, to the wives of the sergeants on the permanent staff who may go abroad being permitted to accom-

pany in addition to the six women per one hundred
allowed by regulation.—I have, &c.

                    " JAMES SIMPSON, *D.A.G.*"

On the ninth of February, the service companies,
about to proceed on foreign service, were finally
selected and told off. The number of those who
had volunteered obliged us to leave behind with
the depôt a large proportion of volunteers, who
were held liable to be called upon at any time to
resume their places in the companies abroad, if
thinned by casualties or required by any other
exigency of the service. From this time to the
day of embarkation, the efforts of the commanding-
officer, zealously and efficiently seconded by the
adjutant and quartermaster, were absorbed in per-
fecting the discipline of the regiment, and in anti-
cipating every possible contingency that could bear
on the approaching embarkation, and in studying
every portion of equipment, however minute, that
could be likely to tell on the comfort of the soldier
in his novel position on board ship. Before, however, leaving their native shores the men were
destined to become eye-witnesses of a small portion
of those horrors that were sown broadcast at that
fearful juncture over the battle-field of the Crimea.
On the morning of the tenth a large Government
steamer was reported to be off the Spit, freighted

with invalids, and a fatigue party of our men were told off and mustered on the jetty in the dockyard, for the purpose of transporting them to the hospital. On being drawn up they found the lieutenant-colonel already on the spot, and under his orders prepared for the performance of their novel duties. On one side of the jetty were arranged a row of wooden cots, made on the principle of hand-barrows, and to each of these four men were told off, two as bearers and the remaining two as a relay, and leather slings were provided for each carrier. Parties of six were then appointed for the purpose of bearing a peculiar kind of cot which had been already sent on board the vessel. After a short delay a small steamer belonging to the dockyard slowly rounded the point, and moved silently and solemnly to the jetty. Every eye was turned towards her. On her deck was ranged a row of white coffin-looking objects each covered with a sheet. The vessel was then carefully made fast to the shore, and six sailors, raising one of the mysterious sheeted forms tenderly on their shoulders, carried it carefully from on board and deposited it on the jetty. The sheet was then withdrawn, and disclosed the calm marble visage of a wounded man cleanly shrouded in his narrow cot of deal, with his hair and flowing beard decently arranged, and a strange, calm, proud, passive expression in

the eye, a type singularly characteristic of each
individual of this gallant helpless band. As the
six sailors returned on board to renew their task,
six soldiers took their places, and with all possible
care raised their burthens on their shoulders and
proceeded with it to the general hospital. After
landing these, the badly wounded, a second party,
consisting of such as were able to leave the vessel
on foot, supported by the friendly sailors, were
laid carefully on the cots prepared for them, and
were conveyed hand-barrow-fashion after their
comrades.

It was my fate, shortly afterwards, to be placed
on a board of inquiry to examine the stores and
food provided for these grievously wounded men,
some of whom were on their deathbeds. We
found that in this newly-erected model hospital,
constructed without regard to expense, there was
not a single bath-room. That the kitchens were
so far removed from the wards that the offer of a
nobleman to supply the sick with game from his
estate was rejected, on the discovery that from the
position of· the kitchens in relation to the wards it
could not be brought to the patients sufficiently
warm to be of service to them. The wine, arrow-
root, tea, and porter, were of the most shameful
description, and more adapted to induce disease
than to avert it; and the cooking for above 300

patients was performed by a solitary pensioner quite innocent of any culinary skill, assisted by a single scullion more ignorant if possible than himself. The report transmitted by us to the general who had ordered the court of inquiry to assemble, tended, I doubt not, to an immediate reform in this most disgraceful department. The care of this large body of sick and wounded soon devolved almost exclusively on the surgeon and assistant-surgeon of our regiment, and the manner in which their arduous duties were discharged elicited a public recognition of their conduct, both as regards their skill and attention to the severe surgical cases which filled the wards, and the general regularity and cleanliness of the hospital at large.

CHAPTER IX.

THE time now.began to draw near for the Royal
Blanks to bid adieu to their old haunts, the scenes
of drill and pipeclay, fun and frolic. Rumour
followed on rumour. Now a gigantic steamer,
expected daily with invalids, was engaged to take
us off. Now a mighty man-of-war, lying idle at
the Spit, was under orders to remove her lower
deck guns, to give us room and verge enough, and
bear us away in style. At last an old sailing
transport arrived, and having been duly inspected
and proved wanting, left with some detachments
for the Crimea. On the twenty-first of February,
we were finally inspected by the general, and
nothing now remained but to await the signal to
embark. While we were thus on the tip-toe of
expectation, down came a sudden order to our
friends, the Red Roses, to hold themselves in readiness to be off immediately on board the steamer

Calcutta. I must here inform the reader that while these busy scenes had been enacted in the barrack-yard of the Royal Blanks, our friends of the Red Rose had been seized with a like fit of patriotism, and the Government, nothing loth, acceded to their request. They were not, however, as yet so forward as ourselves in their preparations, and had no idea of embarking for some weeks. Down came this order therefore suddenly as a bombshell, and in its explosion scattered the authorities. The general began inspecting; the town-major issued orders; the deputy quarter-master-general did something in the same line; the deputy adjutant-general followed suite. The colonel came down on the adjutant, and the adjutant gave no peace to the barracks in general, and the captains discoursed choleric words, and the privates rank blasphemy. Then along the electric wire flashed the intelligence to the big tailor in London, and the big tailor roused up the little tailors, and such a heating of geese, and flashing of bright needles, and packing of bales and barrels, and all for the honour of the Red Roses, hath not been heard of before or since in Tooley Street. Then was the accoutrement-maker badgered, and the tongue of the accoutrement-maker's wife loosened. At length the contractor handed over his bales to the porter, and the porter to the trucks, and the trucks to a fatigue party a hundred miles away, and the Red Roses marched on board with flying colours, and the Royal Blanks, in spite of feeling a little sore at being jilted of the honour of being the first militia regiment to embark for foreign service, gave them three hearty cheers, as on a bright Sunday morning, the fourth of March, they steamed out of harbour.

The long-anticipated hour at length arrived, and on the morning of the sixteenth of March, a crowd collected in the narrow lane outside the still closed gates of the barracks, awaiting the appearance of the Royal Blanks. The night before, although the men had been left entirely to themselves, they had returned from their farewell carousals with great regularity, and no absentees had to be routed up to complete the ranks, as they stood in column of companies, and were told off for the last time in the dingy old square of the Clarence Barracks. Beneath the portico of the mess-room stood the ensigns with the colours in their hands uncased, and surrounded by the accustomed guard of sergeants with fixed bayonets. Near them stood the colonel and lieutenant-colonel ready to fall in in front of the regiment, and march at the head of it to the steamer. At length all preliminaries being completed, the regiment wheeled into line, and a short pause, full alike of silence and excite-

ment, was succeeded by the clear ringing word of
command. The muskets, with their serried pride of
bayonets leaped with a flash to the shoulder, the
band struck up a lively tune, the heavy doors wheeled
back on their hinges, and the Royal Blanks issued
forth amid the cheers of the populace. Half-a-mile's
march through crowded streets, with farewells,
jokes, cheers, and shaking of hands on all sides,
brought us to the tall dark closed gates of the
dockyard. There was no need however of halting.
The huge portals rolled back as by magic, and the
long line of armed men, somewhat disarranged by
their late pressure among the crowd, found themselves in the wide, silent area of Her Majesty's
dockyard. What a change! As the echo of the
closing doors came faintly from the rear, it seemed
as if we had bidden a final adieu to our all of
private life, with its joys, sorrows, hopes, and re-
sponsibilities. As we passed on, the shadows of the
huge frowning massive buildings fell on us with a
quiet chill. Her Majesty's policeman gazed at us
for a moment, and as though ashamed of having
honoured us so far, turned away and paced his wonted
beat, wary and solemn. Her Majesty's convicts
paused as they stooped to grasp a massive log, and
leered at us with a stealthy scowl or sinister grin.
Her Majesty's artificers faced us as we passed with
a glance of curiosity, and then resumed their tasks

as though we were no business of theirs. At length we halted in line, beneath the shadow of the tall black hull of the steamer, and, after a short pause, the men ascended, company by company, on deck. Now commenced a scene of apparent confusion, and which would have been confusion in earnest, had not the men engaged in it been well disciplined, and all difficulties carefully anticipated. Each captain, assisted by his subalterns, marched his company to an allotted space between decks, and his first care was to superintend the fixing firmly, in a range of racks erected for the purpose, the musket of every man in his company. Each soldier was provided with a sea-bag in addition to his haversack, and into this he now proceeded to place his coatee and chaco, and arrayed himself in his light forage cap and his shell-jacket, which was covered by a short frock reaching to the thigh. To every man was then served out a tin can and plate, and a pair of blankets; and a place for sleeping, or rather stowing himself away, was marked out for him and explained. By mid-day every thing had been brought into a very decent state of order, and at one o'clock the men ate their first ship-dinner, well cooked and in comfort. The afternoon was passed in settling all the minor arrangements, and the officers were glad enough when the time arrived to partake of their first dinner in their new home, and turned in early to sleep off the fatigues and excitement of the day. A walk through the lower decks at this hour was amply repaid by many amusing sights, Jack Tar assisting Johnny Raw in his efforts to secure his first night's rest; and many a lecture, accompanied with practical illustrations on the hammock in general, together with the manner of slinging it, getting in and out of it, basking at full length in it, or snoozing cozily in a curl, might have been heard delivered in all the raciness of naval phraseology, and received with a look of puzzled curiosity.

CHAPTER X.

In corroboration of what I have written, and in common justice to the corps, I here insert, in a separate chapter, copies of the general orders issued during the latter period of our stay at Portsmouth; more especially for the perusal of such of my professional readers as may feel sufficiently interested to desire to test the truth of my narrative.

Deputy-assistant Adjutant-general's Office,
Portsmouth, 23d February 1855.

SIR,—I have it in command from the major-general commanding the South-western District, to convey to you that, having inspected the Royal —— Militia, he is happy in having it in his power to report most favourably of the regiment.

The major-general, judging from the short acquaintance he has had with the corps, inclines to the opinion that the interior economy is very good.

The regimental and companies' books particularly well kept, and the system followed in the management of the men must be good, if judged by their general excellent conduct, a fair criterion, as a rule liable to few exceptions.—I have the honour to be, &c.

A. A. NELSON, Captain,

D. A. A. General.

Lieut.-col. Lord M.

Portsmouth, 22d February 1855.

SIR,—I have the honour to report, for the information of the General Commanding-in-chief, that I yesterday made an inspection of the Royal —— Militia, and am happy to have it in my power to report most favourably of that regiment. The system appears remarkably good throughout. The regimental and companies' books particularly well kept. The arms and accoutrements are complete; but an armourer is evidently required, some of the locks being stiff, and showing either that they do not fit or are badly put on. It strikes me, from what I have seen of the officers, that their *esprit de corps* is excellent. Lord M—— is evidently a most zealous officer, and the staff and company's officers appear anxious for the efficiency and well-doing of

E

the men. Of the conduct of the men as a body I
can report in the highest terms.—I have the
honour, &c.

H. W. BRETON,

Major-general Commanding.

The Adjutant-general, Horse Guards.

Horse Guards, 24th February 1855.

MY LORD,—In forwarding to you a copy of
Major-general Breton's report of the inspection of
the Royal —— Militia, I am directed by the
General Commanding-in-chief to request you will
communicate to the regiment his Lordship's entire
satisfaction at its discipline and efficiency, at the
soldier-like manner in which it has performed the
responsible duties of the important garrison of
Portsmouth, and the general good conduct that has
marked its residence there. . These results are most
creditable to the manner in which you have administered the command of your regiment, and the
attention to their duties shown by both officers and
men.—I have the honour, &c.

G. A. WETHERALL,

Adjutant-general.

The Lord M.

Portsmouth, 16th March 1855.

DISTRICT ORDER.

In taking leave of the Royal —— Militia, the Major-general requests Lieutenant-colonel Lord M—— will make known to all the men how pleased he has been with their excellent conduct while in garrison, more particularly in regard to cases of absence without leave, the average daily number of which has been very small indeed. So far as the Major-general has been able to observe, the interior economy of the regiment appears good in every respect. The embarkation of the corps has been carried out with all the regularity and absence of defaulters, upon which the Major-general fully counted, and is so much the more praiseworthy, inasmuch as the men were trusted with their full liberty to the last, notwithstanding which, not a man was absent, nor one intoxicated. Major-general Breton thanks Lord M——, the officers, and non-commissioned officers, for the zeal and attention with which their various duties have been carried out. It is very gratifying to him that he is enabled to forward to the General Commanding-in-chief so favourable a report of this excellent regiment.

By order,

A. A. NELSON, Captain,
Dep. A. A. General.

War Department, 7th April 1855.

MY LORD,—I have the satisfaction to transmit to your Lordship a copy of a letter from Major-general Breton, bearing his testimony of the good conduct and discipline of the Royal —— while stationed at Portsmouth, and on its embarkation for foreign service. The high state of discipline of this corps is owing to the activity and energy of Lieutenant-colonel Lord M—— and the officers under his command, and it affords me great pleasure in communicating to you so satisfactory a result of their efforts.—I have the honour, &c.

PANMURE.

The Lord Broughton, G.C.B.

Portsmouth, 16th March 1855.

SIR,—In transmitting the returns of the troops embarked on board the troop-ship Resistance, as also those who have been this day embarked on board the steamer Crœsus, I have the honour to request that you will be so good as to bring to the notice of the General Commanding-in-chief, that the Royal —— Militia embarked in the most perfect order, not a man being absent or a single case of drunkenness; and as a mere act of justice to this corps, I would beg further to report, for the information of Viscount Hardinge, the excellent conduct of this regiment during the time they have been quartered in this garrison. There has been no offence of a serious nature, and although for the last month under all the excitement of anticipated embarkation from day to day, the returns show barely an average of one per cent. of absentees without leave daily.

It is fully evident to me that the corps is in excellent hands, Lord M——, the lieutenant-colonel in command, being a most zealous officer, and merits my unqualified praise.—I have, &c.

H. W. BRETON,
Major-general Commanding.

The Quartermaster-general.

Horse Guards, 20th March 1855.

SIR,—I have the honour to transmit to you for the information of the Secretary of State for the War Department, the enclosed copy of a letter, reporting in highly favourable terms on the conduct of the Royal —— Militia, during its service at Portsmouth and on its embarkation, and to acquaint you that the General Commanding-in-chief has great pleasure in forwarding to his Lordship a report bearing such honourable testimony to the good conduct and discipline of the corps while it was stationed at Portsmouth, and on its embarkation.— I have, &c.

C. YORKE,
Military Secretary.

To Col. Mundy.

CHAPTER XI.

THE morning of the seventeenth opened in damp and gloom; but, in spite of the weather, men and officers were early on deck, and the ladies, in defiance of sloppy planks and slippery ladders, showed their fair forms, veiled in capes and waterproofs. The scene on deck was busy and confused, and not exclusively nautical. The indefatigable ship-broker, redolent of "the Hard," was in attendance, taking a few last orders and messages, and sending his myrmidons flying right and left in quest of such small articles as had been forgotten. At length, at a word from the captain, he stept ashore, the companion ladder was withdrawn, the gangway closed, the cables that bound the ship to the jetty cast loose, and the last tie between us and our native shore was now gone. So very slow and still was our movement at starting, that it seemed scarcely credible that this strange mysterious motion, this throb of silent mighty power, should never cease; till, through calm and tempest, ripple and foam, it would calmly, but resolutely, cleave its way, and leave us some thousands of miles beyond hail of all we held dear. In spite of the rain, which now began to steal down thickly, the band, which had been mustered on deck, began to play cheerily and loud. "Auld lang syne," "The girls we left behind us," "Cheer boys, cheer," and other appropriate tunes, rang through the driving mist, till we had cleared the entrance of the port, and neared Southsea Castle. These demonstrations were not lost on our friends ashore, and many a fair arm protruded from the casement and waved an adieu, and many a kerchief and mimic flag telegraphed a farewell signal from the more distant windows. The sea had now begun to run high, and both wind and rain to increase, and a circumstance here occurred which threw an additional gloom over our prospects. A boat containing a single man was being towed in our wake, and the time had now arrived to take it in. The tow-line was consequently hauled short, and, alas! either from some mistake in regard to the velocity of the vessel, or some mismanagement, on which it is now idle to speculate, the boat was drawn under water, the poor fellow washed overboard, and left struggling among the waves. In vain was a life-preserver thrown overboard; in vain was a boat lowered. Though a good swimmer, yet encumbered by a waterproof overdress, and swamped by a heavy sea, we saw him gradually beaten down beneath the surface, within a few hundred yards of the beach. He made neither cry nor sign that we could detect. This was a sad beginning to our voyage, and it took days before many of us recovered the shock; and some few muttered, Ha! this comes of embarking on a Friday.

I will not nauseate the reader with any attempt to re-tell the hundred times told tale of a first week at sea. Suffice it, that in spite of heavy weather, and winds dead ahead, we sighted the Lizard on the afternoon of the eighteenth, and then all was sea and horizon. Sadly circumscribed were human sights and sounds. Pallid cheeks, trembling limbs, doleful sighs, gasps presaging the dread crisis, and a Jacobite mania for the steward. The few that held on with an appetite waxed proud, and mixed their grog with an air. Some affected the deck in spite of wind and wet, each with his favourite panacea. The amount of biscuit that one contrived to munch was incredible, but at length he made his way to the bulwarks, a perfect cornucopia, showering plenty among the fishes. My friend of the brandy-and-water cure disappeared first, but whether Neptune or alcohol had been his chief vanquisher, deponent knoweth not. One affected a swaggering air of nonchalance, but perished early in his pride; while another persisted in his method of cure with a pertinacity that did him honour. In steadiness of vision lay his hope of safety; so wedging himself into a corner, he stretched the lids of two large blue eyes to their fullest extent, and fixing them on some chosen spot, like a rifle-man on the bull's-eye, allowed them to revolve with the motion of the vessel, like the bead on a level. Pale he waxed and sulky, but I never before beheld such antagonistic sensations as helplessness and determination so strongly imprinted at once on the same face.

On the morning of the nineteenth, a poor corporal was found dead in his hammock. It was supposed that he had been taken off by a fit. On the same day, the lieutenant-colonel, standing by the gangway, read the solemn service of the dead, while below, swathed decently in his hammock, and covered by the folds of the Union Jack, the corpse lay stretched on the hatch gratings; and on a signal, at that portion of the service when the coffin is lowered into the grave, two sailors gently raised the corners, and the body slid feet foremost into the deep. Two young and sickly infants were subsequently received into the same fathomless tomb, and, with God's blessing, the list of casualties for the entire voyage was complete.

A spanking gale in the Bay of Biscay tried once again the nerves and stomachs of the convalescents, who, from the abyss of the cabins of despair, had floated lightsomely to the surface of the deck, and the night of the twenty-first was a wide-awake nightmare of horrid creaking, groaning, and crashing. Often have I, in times gone by, listened with a strange merriment to the unwonted locomotion administered to inanimate objects by the rising force of a brisk gale. After a little lively clatter, and a hen-roost sort of clucking among the crockery, some more adventurous and rotund article, a salt-cellar, for instance, or a pot of bloaters, would issue, scape-goat-fashion, from its allotted precincts, and darting on the floor play a castanet jig of its own composing, and dart about with the agility of a cracker,—an occasional crunching sound among his comrades, still at home on the shelf, apparently testifying their approbation. Then the bear's-grease-pot of some whisker-cherishing ensign would slide glibly from its resting-place over his berth, and, taking its lid for a partner, whirl and gyrate as if the demons of the storm were playing at spin-halfpenny with it; but the real Tam o' Shanter-like glory of the revel was never complete, till, urged by unwonted motion, some staid huge mass of furniture, that had been fixed like a gouty invalid to a Bath chair, broke from its lashings, and, after a warning scrape or two to try the footing, dashed boldly at once into the troubled arena like a rhinoceros venturing into a quadrille. Then would arise the cry for help; then would the steward, the steward's man, and the cabin-boy, rush to the rescue. Next a burst of oaths, short, emphatic, and to the purpose—a silent concentrated struggle like a life-contest between a gigantic madman and his keepers—victory—tighter cords—a farewell curse of satisfaction, and again the jig between the salt-cellar and grease-pot livelier than ever.

This, and more, kept me on the *qui vive* till morning brought me on deck, and before evening the waves had subsided, and, tempted by a promised view of the scene of the victory of Trafalgar, the denizens of the troubled cabins reappeared on deck. We looked on a wild waste of waters, and were told it was Trafalgar; but were none the less content, and looked more proudly on the old flag as its tricoloured bunting reclined peacefully on the cabin sofa.

We had now fairly entered the straits. The Barbary coast rose bleak and ruggid on our right. Above us, a signal of our entrance into a brighter clime, an awning was stretched over the poop, and as an earnest that henceforth pleasanter hours were in store for us, the band fell in and played a selection of lively airs and dances. The sun was just sinking as we first caught sight of the famous rock, and as we passed within a mile of its "castled steep," the mighty mountain-keep loomed dim and giant-like in the dusk. The heat began now to increase sensibly, and the metallic, sun-smitten, rock-bound coast of Barbary seemed to encoil like a salamander the glowing waters of the Mediterranean. The Bay of Tunis was now pointed out, and subs fresh from school gazed wondering on the site of Carthage.

Little but what had told of the grand and savage had as yet gladdened our eyes, and it is difficult to make one, who has never passed a week on the world of waters, comprehend the sensations of delight we all experienced on finding ourselves, on the afternoon of the twenty-sixth, coasting along within a mile of the shore of the pretty little island of Pantellaria. The sun shone brightly on the tiny town, that, climbing a steep ascent, rose pyramid-shaped from its bright bay where a few vessels lay at anchor; a time-worn fortress tower; a tall white spire; a little maze of white glittering streets; a suburb with smart-looking houses of white stone, adorned with cupola and balcony, and set in olive and orange groves, and the verdure of cultivated land. Our vessel fairly heeled as its living freight crowded the starboard bulwarks each with some remark on the strange-looking sunny spot; but when a veritable man appeared quite distinctly walking down the principal street, taking it easy on his two legs, just as one of ourselves would perambulate the pavement of little Pedlington, the furor he produced, and the battery of glasses he brought to bear on his unconscious person, were scarcely to be exceeded by the entrance of a Kean or a Kemble on the stage in the palmiest days of the drama. Whoever was lucky enough to possess a telescope was soon glad enough to give it up, such a torrent of questions was poured upon him from all quarters. The privates seemed to forget cribs, cabins, confinement, and ship's rations, and to inhale country odours, and ramble among rural sights and sounds. A glance at the Gazetteer informed us that this little island is famous for its olives and honey, and a place of transportation for Sicilian convicts. To stimulate the joyousness of our feelings we surrounded the band on deck, and as we glided by it, too swiftly as it seemed, bade it farewell in a merry waltz.

The next morning, on ascending the deck, we found ourselves coasting along a low table-land of rock-bound shore, the quarry-like edges fringed with a narrow riband of brilliant green. This we found was the island of Gozo, the Patmos of St

John, according to some, and the Island of Calypso according to others, and twin-sister of the renowned Malta. As we continued our route, the central country became somewhat more elevated above the coast, and presented to the view some neat cottages and smiling gardens, and a large white building surrounded by a grove of trees, the remains, we were told, of an extensive botanical garden, instituted mainly on the speculation of raising silk from the denizens of the mulberry trees with which it was largely stocked; but the scheme was a failure as a commercial enterprise.

The veriest sluggards left their berths by times that morning, and as the last sleeper came on deck, the larger, but less fertile island, was under our bows. Nothing very remarkable distinguished the aspect of this spot of world-wide fame; but when at nine A.M. we cast anchor within the harbour of Valetta, the dullest among us was bound to confess that the scene around us was one of strange grandeur and surpassing interest. Imagine a basin of water of intense blue, smooth as a polished sapphire, and then surround it on every side, except at a single small outlet, with masses of yellowish-white stonework glittering tier on tier. The solid rock-hewn battlement, its gigantic foot laved by the rippling waters, with its mural crown of antique turrets, and its masonry pierced and fretted with case-

mated battery, loop-holed watch-tower, and all
the inventions and appliances of defensive warfare
varied by the recurring changes and necessities of
four hundred years of mortal strife. Above, and
clinging like the lowly parasites of the gigantic
Mora-tree of the South American forest, rose light
and graceful forms of varied architecture. Palaces,
arcades with tropic plants waving among their
graceful arches, strange-shaped, yet not inelegant
structures, whose object none could guess. The
dome of a noble temple—the tapering spire of an
English church—a Grecian palace destined to receive that Emperor of all Emperors, Napoleon,
during his brief hour of sway over this key of the
Mediterranean. Uncouth barges, gay with gaudy
paint, plied unceasingly to and fro. On our right
lay the long black hull of a merchant steamer, her
deck crowded by the swarthy figures of a detachment of French invalids returning to La belle
France with their wounds and their glory. The
spirit-stirring strains of a regimental band echoed
along the winding road, as the gallant Buffs, just
landed from the transport Emeu, disappeared
beneath the entrance gate, soon to re-embark and
be hotly engaged in the Crimean struggle.

A party of our officers soon obtained leave to go
on shore, and a merrier squad, and one more agog
for fun, never started on a spree since the days of

Johnny Gilpin. Imagine us leaping like a shoal of middies on the white calcined beach, the devil, in the shape of an unpaid boatman, seizing the hindmost. We stood a moment agape at a row of two-wheeled vehicles harnessed each to a huge mule, the which to describe would be a task for an antiquarian, and compared to which the celebrated Shem, Ham, and Japhet gig, as described by his Reverence Sidney Smith, and supposed to have been discovered on Mount Ararat on the subsidence of the waters, must have been a new invention. Now up a winding milky way of limestone across a white fosse glowing like a furnace, with a fresh green-spreading, fruit-laden fig-tree clinging to its sultry bosom unsinged, a verdant miracle. Then strange, abrupt alleys, with tall dazzling houses on each side, and little limestone statuettes for sale in the windows. At last the unexpected haven of a spot of level ground, and a drawing forth of hand-kerchiefs and doffing of hats, in a ring of strange beggars jabbering a mixed jargon of languages in the strangest of rags, and before us was the vast open doorway of the most magnificent temple of the East, the Cathedral of St John. A huge heavy curtain draped its entrance, shrouding its hallowed gloom from the vulgar glare of the streets. Two misshapen ghoules, fighting savagely, and grinning and jabbering like monkeys, were the guardians of

F

this entrance; but in the heat of the squabble we passed through unfleeced by fees, and met a swarthy ecclesiastic hurrying forward to anathematize the combatants. It was not without a feeling of awe that the giddiest among us found himself standing within the vast vaulted interior of this magnificent temple of world-wide fame. It was not alone the barbaric pearl and gold, mingling with all that is costly in decoration and quaint in ancient carving, that incrusted the vast circumference, and gloomed in heraldic blazon beneath our feet, but the very air felt burdened by the shadows of the mighty past, and dim visions of armed knight and mitred priest seemed to wave us off and deprecate our heretic intrusion on their repose amid the memorials of their departed glory. It is not my purpose to attempt a description of an edifice the bare enumeration of whose wonders and costliness would fill a volume. Suffice it that after a short and exciting survey of magnificent shrines, statuary by celebrated sculptors ancient and modern, gloomy vaults, and thrones of purple and gold, we issued forth once more into the full glare of day. Then came a visit to a jeweller with his host of temptations in coral, pearl, and lava. The ladies in ecstasies, the gentlemen looking graver, with a severe *pater familias* expression of countenance. Then a palace, more curious than grand, with stores of cumbrous artillery of a bygone era; knights helmed and plumed, and glittering rows of storied armour. The cuirass torn and ripped by the iron balls of the infidels, and casque dinted by mace and sabre in the wars of the cross and crescent. Strange specimens of ordnance in leather, brass, and wood, and branded each with some quaint tradition. The sword of some doughty knight, and the ball that had shivered it to the hilt.

A peep from the window by one of our party elicited an exclamation that soon brought the whole of us to the same spot, and there below us, along the pavement of a street as narrow as a lane in Devonshire and as deep as a fosse, was a sight that made us forget for a moment the glories of priest and soldier and mediæval pomp. The whole area of the street was one green line of the most delicious vegetables, fruits, and flowers. The words " green peas" burst simultaneously from the lips of at least two-thirds of the party. The remaining third, which was feminine, exclaimed " La! ·what flowers! " After a minute's gaze at this novel and refreshing sight, we descended again into the hot open, passing a Highland sentry, and careering down the steep straight narrow High Street, surveying with wonder the lanes that branched from it at right angles, almost perpendicular, and com-

posed apparently of a succession of steps formed of
slabs of white stone, thin and broad enough to
permit a horse to climb them. So dazzling was
their glow of burning white that the imagination
reverted to Jacob's ladder, steep and shining in the
vision; but there were no angels here, and the
temperature suggested a very different termination
to the ascent. A kind of café in French fashion,
but rather dingy and crowded, now received us hot,
hungry, and reckless, and strange cates, ices,
liqueurs, lemonade, and brandy figured largely and
promiscuously in the bill, and in such glee was the
male portion of the party on reissuing into the
streets, that the ladies found it necessary to relieve
guard over the pockets, or the tradesmen might
have reaped a goodlier harvest. Now for a visit to
the market, and we were soon luxuriating among
magnificent piles of oranges, melons, dates, pumpkins, and pomegranates; while strange fishes, black,
red, and white, floating in shallow tubs, and cursing
their fate, splashed their few inches of tepid water
angrily at us as we stared in their faces. A few
minutes more sufficed to take us to the ship's side,
bearing in triumph a huge tub of oranges for the
wives and families of the soldiers, and for which
we had not paid above four times the proper
value.

At three P.M. we steamed out from the harbour,

and shaped our course for our final destination, the queen of the islands of Greece. Our voyage up to this time had been so prosperous, and the attention and kindness of the captain of the steamer so marked and cordial, as well as the skill and courtesy with which he redressed the grievances and studied the comforts of all on board, that, by the unanimous desire of the officers, a very handsome pair of opera glasses were subscribed for, and presented to him by the lieutenant-colonel with an appropriate address, which was responded to with hearty good-will by the gallant recipient on behalf of himself and his officers. With one consent we made a gala day of it, as being in all probability the last time we should all sit down together to the social meal at the same table. A few toasts were drunk, and " all went pleasant as a marriage bell," and the sun was level with the lustrous blue expanse of the Mediterranean ere we exchanged the festive atmosphere of the cabin for the breezy coolness of the awning-shaded quarter-deck.

The earliest riser, as he ascended the deck next morning, found us gliding along a tranquil sea, with a lovely island lying a short distance, two miles perhaps, on our left. The banks were luxuriantly wooded to the water's edge, and tall white-washed steeples of a peculiar shape, and white cottages and clustered villages, contrasted gaily with the rich verdure. Further inland, successive ranges of lofty hills of irregular and picturesque outline, but clothed to the summits with foliage, and more variously tinted than the lower lands, arrested the rays of the rising planet, which smiled on them like the god their original inhabitants had believed in and worshipped. On the right, some six miles away, rose the grand but rugged peaks of the Albanian mountains. This charming coast was the ancient island of Corcyra—a name now modernized to Corfu, which it first received at the hands of its Venetian conquerors. Fresh as we were from the environs of Portsmouth, we were unanimous in discovering in it a great general resemblance to the undercliff on the southern coast of the Isle of Wight; but the inland scenery was grander beyond all comparison, and there was an almost tropical luxuriance in the waving verdure through which the dark green-pointed cones of the cypress rose in sombre contrast. All eyes were soon directed to a tall object in front, whether rock or castle was dubious as yet in the hazy distance; but at length the lofty summit of the citadel of Corfu, with its lighthouse and telegraph, stood forth clear and defined in its bold and singular outline; its base a rugged and broken mass of rock, with bushes and creepers clinging to its clefts, and with a girdle of fortifications, scarped from the solid granite, or piled by the hand of the engineer, but massive as the rock itself, and crowded at points and angles by watch-tower and guard-house, the iron lip of many a huge piece of ordnance keeping watch and ward through the embrasures, while, floating like a proud but lovely vision on the embattled steep whose might it typified, the bright folds of the banner of St George spread their glories to the fresh breezes of the subject sea. A rugged knoll, upholding on its apex a small clump of fortified buildings, arrested the eye, but it was at a short distance in rear of it that the head of the promontory lifted itself abrupt and bravely to the sky: of yore, no doubt, rugged, and scarred by many a tempest-blast and lightning-stroke, but now so moulded and subdued by the hand of man, so tortured into form and shape by the successive toil of generations of engineers, that its shelving sides, pierced with embrasures and scarred by their lines of approach, assumed the shape of a gigantic and almost circular tower, its apex a platform for cannon, and an abiding-place for the solitary lighthouse and its attendant signal-station.

As we gradually rounded the point formed by this imposing structure, leaving on our left the beautiful little bay of Castades, likened by travellers to that of Naples, the inhabited portion of the citadel became bit by bit developed. The depressed ridge, which united the afore-described knoll to the loftier bluff, was surmounted by a long neat building of pale-coloured brick, almost concealed by a screen of cypresses. This, as we afterwards ascertained, was the military hospital. At the foot of this range of rock, but raised some fifty feet above the sea by a massive wall, was that unmistakable pile of buildings denominated a barrack; and perched here and there, among the cosiest nooks of the rock, were pretty cottages and neat gardens, the fond and well-feathered retreats of the staff and ordnance. Below the lofty sea-wall was a small haven, artificially defended from the waters of the bay by a breakwater, and filled with the white taut rigging of private yachts and a small steamer. Ere our anchor dashed into the water we had passed this little military nest, and the town of Corfu looked down upon us from the left, while on the right lay the low shelving shore of the island of Vido, its centre tapering to a ridge of small elevation, and crowned by a long low line of white fortifications. Who that has ever passed an hour in that charming little bay can ever forget the ring of beautiful objects by which he was enclosed. On a high old time-stained wall, of Venetian build, the winged lion sculptured on its surface, broken into a quaint variety by loopholed and embattled parapet, studded with antique pepper-box towers, rises the town of Corfu, a conglomerate mass of houses, pile upon pile, in picturesque confusion, with here and there an antique fantastic belfry, with a gaudy weathercock and cross. On an angle facing the citadel lies the small but thickly shrubbed garden of the palace, with a winding stair connecting it with the sea, and a bathing-house at its foot. Above it, stands conspicuous the rear and offices of the palace of the Lord High Commissioner of the Ionian Islands, a large commodious structure, imposing rather from its size and elevation, than from the foreign aid of ornament. A photograph alone could adequately portray the mazy mass of roof and turret, window and balcony, paint and plaster, of the town of Corfu.

Perched on a rocky uneven surface, and with no apparent outlet of street, each house is built on the proprietor's own conception of size, height, colour, shape, and material. Here a crumbling old ruin, once a Venetian palazzo. Here, a house so thin and tall, so white and green, that it would seem transposed from a child's toy-box. Here a handsome shapely building of a mellow colour, and adorned with a stone balcony; and here again, a tiny chapel, with soiled whitewashed belfry, and wreaths of evergreen fading on its walls. Beneath

the wall a small tongue of land protrudes into the
sea, and contains a stunted chapel, cuddling a dingy
group of houses, from one of which projects a jetty
of wood for the accommodation of bathers. Further
on, looking still to the left, a large bay, studded
with the sails of merchant vessels, and surrounded
by quays and official-looking buildings, marks the
position of the mercantile portion of the town; and
just at the rear of it, a second tall buttress of rock,
with its line of barracks at the base, and ribbed
with angular masses of fortification to the very
summit, frowns over the city and bay. A long
reach of water, with woodland hills crested with
white detached houses, sloping to the beach, or
jutting over it in bold headlands, carries the eye
along its extended vista, reposing gladly on its
bosom of molten purple, spangled with the vivify-
ing accessaries of fisher-craft, yacht, and steamer;
but on the right, the bold, majestic mountain of
St Salvador swells from the sea, " and midway
leaves the storm ;" and the vast sterile coast-line of
the Albanian mountains, with their canopy of snow,
and shifting hues of rose and azure, completes the
framing of this delightful picture.

Such were my first impressions of these favoured
localities with which we were destined to become
so familiar. The first boat that approached us was
a neat four-oared gig, with an union-jack in the

stern, and the sanatà officer stept on board, and
after welcoming us to our new station, and satisfy-
ing himself that we had a clean bill of health,
rowed back, and was succeeded by the deputy-
quartermaster-general and other military authorities, and it was settled that the regiment should
not disembark till the next day. A good ration of
fresh meat, with fruit and vegetables, reconciled
the men to this short detention, and the decks of
the vessel were crowded, at early dawn, on the
morning of the thirtieth, with a body of men busily
employed in the duties of a soldier's toilet, and
assisting each other in buckling on their knapsacks
and getting their accoutrements into order. By
this time a line of huge black barges slowly approached the ship, each towed by two boats, the
rowers of which stood upright in them, and faced
the bow, thrusting the oar forward, instead of pulling it towards them as in England; a common
method of rowing here, when the boat is weighty,
or has anything in tow. Our men now fell in by
companies on the deck, and descended carefully
into the barges, which made at once for the shore,
the band playing "Rule Britannia" and "Cheer
boys, cheer." A few minutes sufficed to bring the
whole of the barges into a narrow canal called the
castle ditch, a line of water which separated the
citadel from the esplanade. On the left rose a

huge grand pile of wall to a great height, the
winged lion of Venice grinning in basso-relievo,
forming its sole relief, with the exception of a few
heavily-grated dungeon-looking windows.   On the
right, a sufficient plot of level ground to serve as a
landing-place, and a site for a range of cottages
and a storehouse or two, was bounded by a wall
equally massive but less lofty than that of the
fortress opposite, but crowned with trees and flowers
instead of battlement and embrasure.   About two
hundred yards onwards, these walls were connected
together by a light plain bridge that communicated with the castle-gate and drawbridge, and
spanned the depth below, resting on a pair of light
but strong supports of masonry.   At the first glance
we seemed so enclosed within the bosom of this
huge fosse that we were at a loss which way to
turn, but were directed to a narrow stone staircase
with an iron balustrade, that led to the heights
above, and the men ascending in single file fell in
in line as they gained the esplanade; and here, for
the first time, the regiment, with band and colours,
was drawn up on foreign ground.   As we embarked
on a Friday, so also on a Friday did we disembark,
an escape from all the authorized canons of ill-luck
so unprecedented, that the fact can only be attri-
buted to the overpowering virtue and discipline of
the Royal Blanks.   One of the first things that at-

tracted our attention was the band of our old friends
and rivals the Red Roses, who fell in in front of us,
and played us into the fort. A few minutes' march,
crossing first the bridge, passing under the castle-
gate and guard-house, and through the archway of
a modern line of barracks, and then a short turn to
the left and the men were halted, arms piled, and
our journey was at an end.

To inflict on my readers the description of the
turmoil, fidget, toil and trouble, of what is techni-
cally termed shaking men into barracks, would be
as tedious almost as the work itself, and insure, I
should imagine, a skipping of pages and a yawn
of ennui. Our task was not a little retarded by the
strange disposition of the quarters themselves. A
large and lofty range of buildings, three stories
high, whitewashed but old and weather-stained,
reared itself at the foot of the rock that rose so per-
pendicularly in its rear, that the two were tied to
each other on the higher stories by a series of small
bridges, communicating with wooden galleries that
ran the length of the masonry of the barracks.
Some natural clefts on the face of the rock, enlarged
by the hands of the engineers, formed a site for
several large, long barn-like buildings, that also
served the purpose of barrack-rooms, and were decorated on portions of their exterior with the remains of antique ornament, denoting them to have

owed their origin to the engineers of Venice. The lower galleries communicated with the ground by a succession of descending slopes, paved in a pattern peculiar to the Venetians, and the surface of the ground was here so uneven, that they continued their descent after reaching the lowest story, and led onward to a collection of buildings which included a canteen, washing, and store-house. In detached rooms of this intricate pile were the men of the Royal Blanks eventually deposited, and found, by sad experience, that thousands of miles of water had not divided them from those ubiquitous foes that infest the midnight rest of the cockney in his dear-loved city, and the sojourner in the inns and lodgings of a seaport.

The difficulties the officers had to surmount in settling the regiment in its new quarters would have been easily overcome had there not been in attendance an anxious and helpless class of non-combatants, for whom they considered themselves bound to find a place of shelter. It has pleased Her Majesty's Government to recognise the necessity of admitting a certain number of soldiers' wives to the privilege of accompanying their husbands, for the purpose of washing linen and other feminine accomplishments, and they even go the length of prescribing the number (six to every hundred)

which are entitled to be borne by regulation on the
strength of the regiment. It has also pleased Her
Majesty's Government to ignore practically the existence of this necessary but helpless class, nor even
in the most recently constructed barracks has the
least provision been made for the commonest demands of decency as regards their separation from
the unmarried soldiers. To find accommodation
for thirty-six married women, whose humble but
clean cottages, so lately left behind, dwelt pain-
fully on their remembrance, and who, many with
a baby in their arms, followed their husbands with
looks of alarm and astonishment, was a task that
baffled our utmost endeavours. Money was of no
avail. Lodgings were not to be had; and the
strange wild garb, flashing eyes, and dark mous-
tachios of the few Greeks who were willing to do
a little traffic in that line, filled the poor creatures
with such terror that they would have preferred a
night in the dormitory of a madhouse. It was not
till near the close of the day that, by the unwearied
exertions of our most able and kind-hearted quartermaster, and the good-nature with which the
men gave up their own beds, and submitted to
much privation, that some temporary accommodation was provided for them.

On leaving the barracks I retraced my steps

across the bridge, and on emerging from the precincts of the castle I found myself in the rear of a
lofty marble statue, on a high ornate pedestal, and
on reading the inscription, found it had been raised
to the honour of Field-marshal Schullemberg, the
not unworthy opponent of Charles the Twelfth, of
cut and slash memory, and who, in the olden time,
at the head of a Venetian garrison, gallantly and
successfully defended this fortress against a powerful Turkish armament by land and sea. The
statue, which is said to be a good work of art, represents the hero in full fig, with a flowing wig
and mantle, and baton in hand. He requires
cleaning, especially about the hair and eyes, but is
otherwise in good condition. The situation selected
for the stout old warrior is certainly a very lovely
one. On his right extends an avenue of acacia,
chestnut, and other flowering trees, planted three
deep, and nestling beneath them, and aspiring to
their lower branches, flourishes a gaudy wilderness
of wild geranium, rose, and gladiola. This delightful avenue, some 200 yards in length, is reserved
for foot-passengers, and is the favourite resort of
nursery-maids of all nations, with their gaily dressed
charges. On his left, a continuation of the same
avenue, but minus the flowers, and now widened
to admit the passage of vehicles, extends till the
eye loses it in a steep descent on its way to Cas-

tades. Strait in his front a double avenue, shading
a broad macadamized road, leads in a direct line to
the entrance of the principal street of the town.
This central avenue divides into two portions the
large space of ground that lies between the castle
and the town, and is generally known as the esplanade. The portion on the right (we are standing
for the nonce in Schullemberg's shoes, remember)
is terminated by the palace, which from this point
of view looks very imposing, flanked on each side
by two lofty arches, and partially veiled in front
by a small garden of flowering shrubs surrounding
a fountain, and the bronze statue of the late Sir
Thomas Maitland, once Lord High Commissioner
of these islands. The space between the avenue
and the palace is set apart for the parade-ground
of the garrison, and the ceremony of guard-mount-
ing. That on the left slopes upward in an uneven
swell, and its apex is crowned by an elegant little
Grecian temple, while the houses of the town close
gradually round it in an irregular curve, meeting
the extreme left of the avenue like the arc of a
bow. Horizontal with the geranium walk, and
forming the opposite boundary of the parade-
ground, though separated from it by a line of
young trees and the carriage-road, is a strait lofty
line of houses, with a colonnade in front sheltering
a paved walk, the Regent Street of Corfu, and it

contains the principal shops, the greater proportion of which are English in their arrangements, and decorated with taste. I will refrain from any further attempts at description at present, and return to my narrative of events.

CHAPTER XII.

WE found the garrison to consist of two of Her Majesty's regiments of the line, the Forty-eighth and Eighty-second, besides our old allies the Red Roses; and both officers and men must ever look back with satisfaction on the cordial feelings which united the different corps, up to the time when the requirements of the service removed our comrades of the line to the seat of war. On the day subsequent to our landing, our officers were entertained at the mess of the Eighty-second, and, two days afterwards, received a similar compliment from the Forty-eighth. On the seventh of April, we were for the first time brought under the notice of the commandant, Major-general Macintosh, being brigaded in quarter-distance columns with the two line regiments and the Red Roses, and marching round afterwards in open column, in slow and quick time. On the tenth, two men-of-war steamers,

Sidon and Leopard, arrived in port, and the two
regiments of the line bade us adieu, and embarked
for the Crimea.

The time of year on which we landed happened
to be a very fortunate one, inasmuch as it gave us
an opportunity of seeing, with eyes fresh from home,
the celebration of their most remarkable religious
fasts and festivities, at which times the people
crowd the streets of their metropolis in their gala-
costumes, and show themselves to the greatest advantage.   On Palm Sunday, which fell this year
on the first of April, occurs the most imposing religious procession that is celebrated in the Greek
Church, and I succeeded in getting a seat at a window which commanded a view of the whole.   I
took up my position a full hour before the time at
which the show was appointed to commence, but
the scene before me was too strange and exciting
to allow of my feeling a moment's weariness.   Below, within a somewhat contracted space, very irregular in shape, and so uneven in surface that the
figures thronging it remained distinct in groups, as
chance had thrown them on the higher or lower
spots of ground, an immense concourse of the
populace crowded restlessly, and climbed, sat, or
lounged, in picturesque confusion.   The windows
of the tall, grotesque houses were also crowded by
their occupants in their holiday attire.   The art of

man never designed a dress more completely picturesque in effect than that of the Albanian. The
snowy kilt, with its ample folds quilled like the
petals of the dahlia, droops gracefully from a jacket
of the finest velvet, scarlet, green, or black, superbly
embroidered with gold thread. The leggings are
of a similar material, and corresponding colour,
also elegantly embroidered, and from the open
sleeve of the jacket the snowy cambric of the shirt
droops like the lawn of a bishop. The scarlet fez,
its top covered with gold tracery, from the centre
of which an ample tassel of blue silk droops heavily,
is placed smartly and jauntily on the head, per-
mitting the curly raven locks to show luxuriantly
below it, and contrasting by the brilliancy of its
colour with the black sparkling eyes and swarthy
visage, whose keenly-cut Grecian contour no whisker is allowed to mar, while a small black moustache, curled tightly upwards, adds a singular
piquancy and fierceness to the expression. A belt
of leather, the material rendered almost invisible
by excess of gold ornament, contains in front a peculiar kind of pouch or nest, smothered also in gold
braid, in which repose in state the wearer's pets, in
the shape of daggers and pistols, beautifully
mounted in silver, and which he is constantly
fingering, with an affectionate look of satisfaction.
With his swaggering gait and waspish waist he

looks the veriest little fighting-cock, with a touch of the golden pheasant.

The dress of the Corfiote Greek, though far inferior to that of the Albanian, is not without a touch of the picturesque. The invariable red fez and blue tassel, which imparts a poppy-bed look of wavy brightness to a moving multitude, is contrasted by a jacket of dark blue, enlivened by a broad white shirt-collar that falls over it. A strange kind of bag, of the same colour and material, serves the purpose of a nether garment, and gives a decidedly Dutch expression to that portion of the human form divine. White stockings, and a curiously shaped shoe of bullock's hide, with the toe pointed upward, and occasionally ornamented on the instep with a mosaic of coloured leathers, completes the costume.

The grotesque splendour of the gala-dresses of the females is much more difficult to describe. Over the head, rather than on it, supported by a kind of frame, and of the showiest colours, white, green, or yellow, is a something between a veil and a head-dress, rising in front so as to shade the face without concealing it, and drooping on the shoulders behind. This structure is seated on the head on large folds of plaited hair, the identical locks that adorned in days gone by the cranium of the grandmother, great-grandmother, and as many ancestral females as the wearer can reckon back to, and which have been handed down as heirlooms in the family, and are destined to be religiously transmitted to the next generation. To give this nest of hair a smart appearance, strips of scarlet velvet are plaited into it. Some of the wives of the richer order of small proprietors wear a jacket resembling those of the Albanians, but the larger portion cover the arm and shoulder with a loose jacket of white calico, allowing the chemise to be seen in front, over which, suspended by a gold chain, is an oval plate of gold, on which is engraven a picture of the Virgin and Child, or some saint or angel. This chemise is frequently covered in turn by a green or yellow gauze kerchief. The comparative wealth and importance of the wearer are advertised by the number and value of the gold ornaments with which these portions of the dress is covered. Gold pins sparkle in the hair, long massive earrings rest on the shoulders, and the number of ornaments shaped like gold coins, and all of the purest metal, that are pendent on the breast, would astonish a London belle. The skirt, which is made of stuff, is worn full, and descends to within an inch or two of the shoe. It is generally black, and bound with bright-coloured riband. An apron of clear white or coloured muslin, from the sides of which flutters a row of long streamers of showy ribbon, completes the costume down to the shoe, which is either white or black, and rather clumsy in make, but barely large enough to support the monstrous silver buckle which almost conceals it. The effect of a moving mass of people in such dresses as these can only be realized by watching the colours of a kaleidoscope in gentle motion.

I must now attempt a description of the procession, which had commenced emerging from a street immediately opposite. A large banner, on a pole at least twenty feet in height, and surmounted by a Greek cross in silver, had already taken up a position, and was evidently awaiting the procession to form in its rear. A man, bareheaded, and clothed in a long tunic of blue linen, and with a red scarf round his waist, had charge of it, and was assisted by two lads in a similar dress. In the rear were three priests in their robes of state, their long grey beards and flowing hair falling over a richly embroidered dress of silk, worked with flowers, in a large and rather gaudy pattern; and among the crowd of priests that walked in review before me that day, I could not observe the use of any distinctive colours, but each seemed chosen according to the fancy of the wearer, green, yellow, and violet, being paramount. I think it highly probable that a Greek archæologist would correct me on this point, and reduce the apparent diversity to some certain rule; but I only pretend to present to the reader the first impressions of a Johnny Newcome, which, after all, are in general the most vivid and interesting. On each side, and in front of the cross, were a crowd of lads and boys, drest chiefly in the blue tunic, and bareheaded, each of whom carried a large wax taper, which they proceeded to light in the face of the midday sun, and dropped gradually into order in two ranks, leaving a broad space between. The faint sound of a distant band now became audible, and the banner borne slowly forward, gave room for a second, and a third, and a fourth, till, as well as I could guess, at least fifty, similarly attended, defiled slowly below me, covering a space of ground of about a quarter of a mile. I should calculate the number of robed priests to exceed a hundred, but the number of attendants who ministered to the procession must have been ten times more numerous. In addition to the banners, which had been contributed from all the chapels contained within the city, and on each of which was a painting of the Virgin and Child, or some saint or saintly legend, a number of crosses, all ornately carved and plated with silver, were displayed aloft, together with a goodly array of circular pillars, white and polished, and surmounted each by a coronal of gold, from within which a flickering light smoked and flaunted, and which added a novel feature to the scene, and were intended, I presume, to represent Brobdignag tapers. The eye began to weary at length with the stately monotony of the spectacle, when the band, the tones of whose solemn march had long been heralding their approach, emerged into view. Sixty musicians, dressed in uniforms of dark blue, with scarlet facings, the tunics ornamented with crimson aiguillettes, and wearing Roman helmets of polished brass on their heads, surmounted by a black horse-hair plume, advanced in military order, and in their rear were a company of priests, more richly decorated than their companions, and among them the archbishop of the island, a fine-featured, intellectual-looking old man, bearing his massive gold pastoral staff in his hand, and with his head crowned with a magnificent tiara of gold, with a cross on the apex. Behind him, under a rich dais supported by priests, was borne what had the exact appearance of a gilt sedan-chair, through the windows of which appeared the mahogany-coloured head of a mummy, the neck awry, and the face falling over the left shoulder, leaving little to be seen on the opposite side but the back of the head, covered with a thick crop of very black hair. This is all that now remains of the martyr St Spiridion, patron-saint of Corfu. At his approach the multitude, which had all along saluted each advancing

banner with crossings and genuflexions, seemed
seized with a more solemn awe, and kneeling in
the dust, with heads uncovered, and eyes cast to
the ground, worked their fingers over their breasts,
in the form of a cross, with such quickness and
dexterity, as to dazzle the eyes of the spectator,
already half-dizzy with the motley show. I for-
got to mention that a slow, monotonous chant,
quite different in its cadence from any in use in the
Latin or Anglican Church, and most disagreeably
nasal in its tone, formed a very unpleasant accom-
paniment to the procession, and I was greatly relieved when the droning became overpowered by
the grand trumpet-notes of the band. In the rear
of all, uncovered, and taper in hand, followed the
aristocracy of the island, some in court-uniforms,
but the majority in a plain evening-dress of black.
The saint was then carried to a rising spot of
ground overlooking the country, from whence he
was supposed to impart his blessing to the olive-
trees, and which is, in truth, the only trouble the
Corfiotes are accustomed to bestow upon them. He
is next taken the whole circuit of the town, and
again replaced in his sanctuary, where he reposes
in gold and silver state, in a stifling atmosphere of
incense, while the flare of numerous lamps glitters
on masses of tawdry ornament, in his own cathedral of St Spiridion. In honour of the day the

guns of the castle thunder forth a salute of twenty-one rounds. A few years ago, the Lord High Commissioner, and principal officers connected with his court, attended this procession in full dress, but that custom is now abolished.

It is a singular fact that the poor saint is not his own master, but the property of a private family, and let out to the Church at a rent of three hundred a-year. The speculation on the ecclesiastical side would appear to be by no means a bad one, for the offerings at his shrine during the time of the cholera exceeded the sum of three thousand pounds. The saint gets nothing of course but a ride round the town.

On the fifth, I had an opportunity of seeing a much more beautiful spectacle connected with the Greek Church. It consisted of a torch-light procession in which the same actors figured, but the effect was far more beautiful. The night was moonless, but the cloudless sky was sown with stars that were reflected on the glassy surface of the bay. As I leant over the rails of my balcony listening to the play of a fountain beneath, I watched the groups below as, one by one, the torch-bearers took up their places in line, facing inwards, with space enough between them for the procession to pass through. It was evident that the spectacle was intended to be one of peculiar solemnity, for

although the restless jabber of the Greeks rustled
forth at times like the sudden rising of a breeze
among dead leaves, yet it was invariably hushed
by a warning hist! that ran like electricity the
whole length of the line. After a time came the
sounds of distant music very slow and solemn.
The drums were muffled, and the tune that of the
Dead March in Saul; and when they turned an
angle and came suddenly into view, they were
marching at funeral pace, while on each side were
ranks of police in a dress of rifle green and crimson caps, and with their arms reversed. The
flickering torch-light glittered on the brass helmets
of the band and the embroidered robes of the priests,
and flashed on the crosses of polished silver and
blazoned banners, while jets of fitful flame, darting
from the golden coronals of the huge white pillars,
added a weird and gnome-like splendour to the
scene. One group struck me as peculiarly beautiful. A gigantic silver cross, elaborately carved and
polished, and reflecting the light of several attendant
pillars, formed the centre of a group of Albanians
in all the pride of their magnificent attire. Their
white kilts shone like silver, and the bright steel
of their drawn sabres glittered on their shoulders,
and each marched as if he were a King Aladdin in
all the bravery of his magic jewels. Albanian
children in the same dress, and holding little

sabres, added much to the fairy-like charm of the group. At last a sort of ark covered with velvet, and representing the holy sepulchre in which the body of our Lord is supposed to rest, preceded by the archbishop, slowly swept by amid the dead silence of the crowd cowering on their knees. While this was passing beneath me, another procession on the opposite side of the bay, at the distance of about four miles, was also taking place, and the twinkling lights, moving in the distance, added greatly to the general effect.

I had said before, that on Saturday the seventh, our regiment took part in the evolutions of a brigade-day; but I omitted to remark that the words of command were rendered at times unintelligible by reason of the confusion and noise that reigned throughout the town. A strange incessant turmoil of smashing and crashing, accompanied by clouds of dust, commenced the uproar. Flights of startled pigeons wheeled over our heads; and the cur-tribe, all bewildered, with tails packed closely between their legs, charged from the streets into the welcome open of the esplanade, the majority yelping, as fresh from recent outrage. Then every bell in the town jangled as if the fiends were tugging at it, and incessant reports of pistols and crackers reverberated along the streets. Was it an earthquake, a revolution, or both together. All we could tell was that we were on parade, and that all curiosity must be deferred till a more suitable opportunity. As it fell to my lot to be present in the island during the time of the next anniversary of this phenomenon, I took the opportunity of becoming a spectator of it, and will describe it at once. In the morning of this day the procession of St Spiridion makes the accustomed circuit, and is intended to typify the entrance of the Holy Ghost. At the close of this procession the body of the saint is replaced in the huge silver coffin which adorns his shrine, and when he re-enters the church, at a given signal the horrid sounds commence, and the inhabitants, for the purpose of showing an outward sign of the inward cleansing of their hearts for the entrance of the Holy Spirit, throw out of the windows all their cracked and useless crockery, as well as dust and ashes. The chief implements broken are certain little jugs of porous clay used for cooling water, and which are calculated to last a year only, on account of the pores becoming clogged by the sediment left in the process of per-colation. To walk the streets at this crisis is of course a service of danger, and I saw a man nearly killed by a blow on the cranium and carried off to the hospital. It is also reckoned a proof of zeal to discharge fire-arms; and in fact, everything seems praiseworthy that tends to increase the general riot

and confusion. I couldn't refrain from a hearty
laugh at a grave, old, corpulent tradesman who
issued from his door with two double-barrelled
pistols in his hands, and then, shutting both eyes,
discharged the four barrels with a devout solemnity,
and forthwith re-entered his house with the air of
a man whose mind had just been relieved by the
performance of some momentous duty. I am now
under the necessity of detailing a practice, so loath-
some and cruel, that I trust the increasing intelligence of the age will soon interfere to suppress it.
No form of religion can possibly inculcate the
practice of cruelty. It is the custom of every
household to provide themselves on this day with
a lamb, and the piteous bleating of these helpless
creatures, shut up in close confinement, afflicts the
ear of the passer by for days previously. As soon
as the commotion begins, these poor creatures are
dragged to the doors and there slaughtered, and
the blood smeared, in the shape of a cross, on each
side of the door-posts. The number of lambs to
be sacrificed at the same time renders it impossible
for all but a very few to obtain the services of
skilled butchers, who, nevertheless, rush about from
house to house all bloody and breathless, and leaving their work half-finished. The majority of
victims who fall into the hands of the ignorant and
unskilful suffer cruelly, and moans, struggles, and

blood render the streets hideous and disgusting. On this day it is also reckoned very devout and Christian-like to revile and persecute the unlucky Jews, who are mobbed and pelted whenever they appear. They of course keep themselves on these occasions strictly to their own quarters, where they are strong enough to hold their own against molestation.

A word here about these Jews, who amount in number to about five thousand, and inhabit a portion of the town set apart for them. On Saturday they may be seen in their Sabbath attire lounging on the esplanade, or strolling with children in their arms into the adjacent country. It is difficult to say whether or no, within the penetralia of their labyrinth of dens, they may possess secret hoards of the barbaric pearl and gold which romance has ever loved to associate with them, and which facts have in many instances confirmed; but here at least, settled among a race whose religious system holds them in a degree of contempt and abhorrence unknown among the other Christian Churches, they assume the outward garb of poverty and degradation. The dress of the women is very plain, consisting of a gown of blue or purple print, with a kerchief folded across the bosom. Ear-rings con- constitute their sole attempt at ornament. The unmarried women wear no covering on the head

H

but its natural one of hair, neatly bound round and fastened in a knot behind. The married invariably conceal it by a coloured handkerchief which is wound tightly round the head and pinned, without showing the ends, or displaying any kind of ornament. As a race I have never seen one so utterly devoid of comeliness. I cannot recall an instance of a really pretty girl among them. Their complexion is invariably of an unhealthy yellow, and, as they approach middle age, a lean and hag-like aspect seems to creep over them like a curse; but in some instances they bloat into a something foul and fat. The men's costume consists generally of a rather tight-fitting dress of a seedy blue of home manufacture, and wretchedly dyed. They are little superior to the women in appearance, and the expression of the generality of their faces is indicative of apathy rather than of cunning. They walk with a peculiarly shambling gait, and present a sickly and attenuated appearance.

CHAPTER XIII.

The gap made in the garrison by the departure of the Forty-Eighth and Eighty-Second Regiments, was supplied by the arrival of the Royal Potteries, who disembarked on the thirteenth. Their helmets of black leather, surmounted by an ornamental spike of polished steel, and white shell-jackets, imparted to them a smart and novel appearance, and made them a favourite regiment on parade—a verdict justified in every respect by the intrinsic merits of the corps. Ably commanded and well-officered, their movements on the drill-ground were correct and steady. Their well-disciplined and orderly conduct caused their departure to Cephalonia, a few months after their arrival, to be regretted by all.

After the embarkation of the Eighty-second we succeeded to their parade-ground, a level spot just within the battlements, and commanding a beauti-

ful view of the Bay of Castades. On your left, at
the entrance, the rock rose steep and rugged. A
few plants of the cactus-tribe and bushes of wild
sage clung to its clefts, and a few wild flowers
found here and there a ledge to rest on ; but at one
spot, a platform near its base gave room for a few
buildings and a pretty little garden, in which an
oleander-tree some twenty feet in height and of
proportionate size, was a perfect flaming bush of
flowers. . Above our heads veered and cawed a
solitary brace of ravens, who had found for themselves a little inaccessible hermitage far aloft in a
black cranny like the key-hole of a dungeon. Conspicuous, at the farther end, was the neat and
appropriate chapel for the use of the garrison,
occupying nearly its extreme width with its plain
but handsome architrave and row of massive
marble pillars. Its interior, cool and commodious,
was adapted for the reception of two entire regiments. The respective bands performed in turn at
divine service, and vied with each other in the
progress made in the science of church music.

On the morning of the ninth of May, while
walking on the bridge that crosses the fosse, I was
witness of a scene that reminded me of our being
in a state of war. A vessel was lying in the harbour in quest of shot and shell for the Crimea, and
large fatigue-parties of our men were busily en-

gaged in transporting loads of shells from the magazines of the fortress to the castle ditch, where a little fleet of barges were waiting to receive them. The shells were carried separately by two men on a hand-barrow, each squatting cumbrously on a cushion of hay, as if doggedly conscious of its own importance. On reaching a level bit of ground on the summit of the wall next the esplanade, a party of artillerymen placed them one by one on a kind of spout, and rolling to the end of it, they dropped the fifty feet with a thud that made the very foundations of the bridge quake, into the fosse on a level with the castle ditch, where they were received by another party and transferred to the barges. It was a strange kind of interest that chained me to the spot as I watched these enormous implements of destruction, poising for a moment as it were, plunge headlong, gathering, as they went, a fearful velocity. At first they half-buried themselves in the solid earth; but some old baulks of oak being placed underneath, they acquired sufficient recoil to send them rolling lazily towards the barges, the timber splintering and smashing under their blows.

On the thirteenth a guard of honour, consisting of our grenadier and light companies, with the band and colours, repaired to the palace to assist at the ceremony of the presentation of an address

from the Legislative Assembly to the new Lord
High Commissioner Sir John Young, who had just
succeeded Sir Henry Ward on his appointment to
the Governorship of Ceylon. We lined the great
entrance-hall, and received with due honours the
Regent, the President, and the members of the
Legislative Assembly as they made their appearance. The Archbishop and a numerous array of
clergy formed an imposing procession. The Roman-
catholic Church was also represented by a bishop,
and, as far as I remember, four priests. An Armenian ecclesiastic, in a handsome dress of black and
violet, was also present; but he must have been a
chance visitor in the island, as the Armenian
Church is quite unknown here. A host of uniforms, staff, infantry, and artillery, flared up and
shed a gala hue round about them.

To a new comer a walk through the streets of
Corfu is very interesting and amusing, and I will
present my reader with a sketch of them before the
charm of novelty has had time to wear away. Two
principal streets cut their way through the town of
Corfu, both taking their rise from the esplanade.
The Strada Reale strikes across to the large gate-
way that pierces the fortified wall on the south of
the town, a broad embattled structure, comprising
a large arch with separate entrances for pedestrians.
The Venetian lion keeps watch as usual in stone

over its portals, and within it a small picture of the
Virgin and Child, carefully enclosed in a little
shrine with a glass front, and with a little lamp
perpetually alight in front of it, exacts an obeisance
from every orthodox passer by. Going through
this gate late at night on duty, I was surprised to
find the whole surface of the ground, with the
exception of a narrow lane in the centre, strewn
with what appeared to be a succession of dark-
coloured bales packed closely and neatly in order
so as to economize space ; but what chiefly took
me aback was the strangest moaning cadence, that,
mingling with a hot steam of essence of garlic,
filled the vaulted roof, and brought vividly to my
recollection a line of poor Hood's ; " a groaning in-
termittent sound like Gog and Magog snoring."
The mystery was soon explained. Each bale
resolved itself into a capote with a Greek in it, and
the groaning and the garlic were his natural noc-
turnal emanations.

The Strada Mercante, which is the longest of the
two, divides the town nearly in the centre, proceeding in a direct line to the market-place, and then
losing its identity in a web of lanes that branch
right and left to Fort Neuf, the quays, and the
Line Wall. Both these streets are sufficiently
wide to admit of carriages passing without crowding on each other, besides allowing a small riband

of pavement on each side.   Many of the shops will
well repay inspection.   Workers in gold and silver
ornaments make a great show, as the gold plates,
pins, and chains, so much in request among the
peasantry, hang glittering within the open window.
From the ceiling are suspended specimens of the
silver and gilt lamps, that depend by chains of the
same material from the roofs of the chapels.   On
entering the shop as a purchaser, the proprietor will
produce from his private store some very elegant
specimens of filigree-work in silver.   The brace-
lets are peculiarly chaste and elegant, and are
generally ornamented with medallions containing
the heraldic symbols of the seven islands.   At the
back of the shop the articles may be seen in course
of manufacture.   A few of the larger shops, especially such as deal principally with the garrison and
the English portion of the inhabitants, affect glass
windows, and an interior arrangement resembling
those at home; but the emporium of the genuine
Greek tradesman partakes much more of an eastern
character.   A huge aperture, in which we should
expect to find a window, but the base of which is
more frequently used by the proprietor as a perch
whereon to squat cross-legged, gives light to a
confined appartment stuffed with wares in great
disorder, and serves in general the purpose of a
work-shop as well as a place of sale.   There is no

better criterion of the temperature than these shops
afford to a student of human nature. It is quite as
unerring and a much less cruel thermometer than
the famous bottle with a frog in it. Suppose, on
passing one of these stores, the inmates are discovered in the furthest recesses, sitting each apart,
blue-nosed, and querulous. Depend on it the thermometer is not much above forty. Should they
be full in view, and working with a gentle clatter
of tongue and tool, set it down as sixty; but should
the chairs be drawn forward or invade the sanctuary
of the pavement, and a sewing and cobbling, and a
hammering and jabbering and gesticulating, be
all in a work together in a merry whirl, then
depend on it it is nothing under seventy in the
shade. The shops of the old Greek tailors took
my fancy as being the most quaint. Spectacles on
nose, and wielding an enormous pair of shears, his
crossed legs quite covered by the ample folds of
that garment to which the designation of "small-
clothes" cannot be applied without a glaring viola-
tion of the truth in the isles of Greece; smothered
almost by numerous pieces of a kind of cloth prepared from goat's hair, with strips of scarlet and
yellow lying about in great disorder, he receives
his customers in a kind of state, and disdains the
smirking fidget of the cockney snip. Hardware
shops are numerous, and their articles of sale very

miscellaneous. A grinding-wheel is generally in full work, and a range of jugs of porous earth and other kinds of pottery is placed in rows outside, while suspended from above hang festoons of instruments of cutlery, among which, the most remarkable is a kind of pruning-knife used in the vineyards which combines the properties of a hatchet and a hook. Confectioners' shops are numerous, but the greater proportion of their contents would not be suitable to an English palate. Sugar-plums of all shapes, colours, and sizes, and made of almost every material, from sweetened dough to plaster of Paris, form the chief of the stock, to which must be added a kind of cake made of honey and almonds crushed into a hard mass, and which I can answer for as most delicious. The tobacconist is generally content with a moderate display; but his window is frequently decorated with a large glass vase full of the curly lamina of the golden weed. Pipe-heads of red clay, and stems of cherry and jasmine, are piled around, set off in the shops of more pretension with Turkish and Albanian ornaments, beads, slippers, and embroidery. What greatly surprised me was the total absence of any indications of that taste for art which was once the joy and glory of their ancestors, those artistic giants, the remnants of whose works laugh to scorn the efforts of our degenerate chisel. A few prints of the lowest degree of execution are the sole efforts of native artists to illustrate the thousand-and-one charms of their beautiful island. As regards the sister art, the only specimens I saw consisted of a basket-load of wretched yellow and green parrots, the rejected trash of the humblest cabin in England whose mantelpiece they have ceased to encumber. Strange that this plaster abortion of a bird, expelled from their soil by the barbarians of the north, should find a place to roost on the classic soil of the east.

Wine-shops are very numerous, but make little outward show. Sometimes the only guide is a bush suspended outside; but signs, both in Greek and English, are occasionally seen, and not a few devote themselves almost entirely to the military, and rechristen the house at the advent of every fresh regiment,—a cheap compliment, which costs but a little paint. I was amused by reading over the door of a hot-looking little hole the following inscription, "The Blankshire Oven," and the interior certainly bade fair to justify the appellation. It is not, however, in the two streets I have already spoken of, or the few others that partake of their characteristics, that the curiosities of a city like Corfu are to be sought. As a tyro in anatomy soon becomes acquainted with a few of the leading veins and arteries of the human body, so an aver-

age Johnny Newcome needs but a short time to
learn to follow his nose through certain lines of
thoroughfare, sufficient for the purpose of the hour;
but as the skilled anatomist only can trace the
devious network of the tissues that permeate the
human body, now branching, now circling, never
ending, still beginning; so let the said Johnny be
once fairly set down among the mazes of the by-
streets, and ere he has threaded them all he will
issue forth a wiser, a wearier, and a warmer man.
Lucky for him that few steps save his own tread
these devious paths.   It gives him room and verge
enough to dodge round the reeking puddles that
settle between the uneven boulders that form the
pavement, save where the rocky ground has itself
been pummelled into a roadway.   Hills and dells
lie front and rear; here a flight of steps, and there
a cul-de-sac, but oftener far the peculiar circling
curve that, diverging constantly into fresh alleys,
and crossed and recrossed in bewildering confusion,
went to constitute the ancient labyrinth.   Females
he sees none; save perhaps a head prying stealthily
from a window, and withdrawn in haste when observed.   A few men of the lower orders glide by
him in silence, and occasionally he finds himself
driven into the friendly shelter of a doorway, while
a donkey, with its uncouth clumsy saddle and pair
of reeking wine-casks, or skins of oil, and driven by

a scowling Greek, trudges wearily along, brushing the houses on each side. Hedged 'in by buildings of great height, deserted almost by the human race, that are wont in our towns at home to tread so busily the like resorts, he looks upward, and sees a double of his winding path in a blue riband of glowing sky, edged with gold on the side on which the sun smites the summits of the lofty walls. What unfamiliar faces do the houses on each side present! Here and there, at long intervals, a something like trade, in the shape of a range of stores; their low, dark interiors crowded with casks, and reeking with lees of wine. Then a veritable hovel, and next to it, soiled with the dust of centuries, its carved balcony weather-stained, and foul with weeds, or cumbered with ragged clothes hung to dry—the tall wreck of a palazzo, once the joyous abode of Venetian splendour. Then again, glaring with white walls and smart green jalousies, a large and roomy home of modern comfort, with a contracted space in rear, half-yard, half-garden, above the jealous walls of which the jagged plume of the banana tells of its eastern clime. At times he falls on a more busy street, wider, and diversified with a shop or two, and a frequent sign that is apt to make the boldest tremble, and pass his tongue across his teeth, viz., a human visage in the grotesque agony produced by a vicious instrument inserted into the mouth, the other extremity grasped by an unrelenting hand, flanked by a naked arm compressed by a ligature, while a stream of blood curves upward in the air. If he require neither shaving, bleeding, nor tooth-drawing, let him pass on and be grateful.

The market, at early morning, is ever a scene of liveliness and interest. A large square building, open in the centre, but roofed in at the sides, to afford shelter to butchers at one part, and poulterers and fishmongers at the other, forms the nucleus around and within which the worthies that buy and sell chaffer and congregate. I will not stop to grow eloquent over the tiny but sweet lamb, small mutton, and lean beef, but take the reader at once to the counter of the fishmonger and poulterer, where the display of glittering sardines, rosy mullet, and a species of mackerel, with an occasional John Dory, and a nondescript or two, make a tolerable show on the leaden slab; and now let us cast a glance on these shiny baskets where congregate the cheaper piscatorium of the poor. "Strange things come up to look at us," tick-bodied, and spider-legged, frilled with spikes, and bearded with suckers, scrambling and squattering, goggling and fidgeting, imps of gluten, that sting and bite, and pinch and spit, and yet, despite of all, are bought and swallowed sauceless, after frying alive on the charcoal. Among then the least disreputable appears the cuttle-tribe, one species of which particularly interested me, on account of his human affinities. When trifled with he defiles you, attorney-wise, with ink, a waterproof-bag of which he cherishes in his heart of hearts, and draws the stopper with a pop. A glance at the vegetables and we have done. A goodly show of beans and brocoli, lettuces, pease, and leeks innumerable, and the never-absent garlic, which so constantly and effectually distils itself in the penetralia of every Greek, that break him or ruin him as often as you will, you will never cease to nose him. Bulbs in this country lose their figures early. The radish, slim and crisp in our northern climes, here swells himself out and apes the beetroot, and gourds and pumpkins, scarlet, green, and yellow, bulge into monstrous shapes. A tribe of bare-legged boys, from seven to seventeen, provided with wicker-baskets, tout about the market as carriers, and as the regulated rate of porterage to any place within the city-walls is somewhat less than one-halfpenny, they are constantly employed, and the activity of their limbs cannot be impeded by the weight of their pockets. Tethered in a row by themselves, and patiently munching a few half-decayed leaves, are a troop of donkeys, mules, and broken-down ponies, each burdened with a rude wooden saddle, quite a load in itself, the coarse, heavy harness, covered with shabby finery, and tags of scarlet and yellow cloth.

The fruit-market is held more in the centre of the town, round a small fountain, and has altogether greater pretension to elegance. Bouquets of flowers are exposed for sale, and oranges, figs, grapes, strawberries, peaches, Java-medlars, pears, plums, walnuts and melons, succeed each other in cheap profusion. The town of Corfu is well supplied with water. Numerous public fountains dispense night and day their clear, sweet, cool streams, and pipes conduct them to the summits of the houses of all who choose to pay for the accommodation. I need not say that this is the result of English enterprise. A splendid spring bursts forth among the mountains that overhang the village of Benitza, distant about seven miles from Corfu. This spring, by dint of pipe and aqueduct, is poured in profusion into the thirsty streets of the town, and all the works connected with it are under the charge of the military engineer department.

I had a good opportunity of inspecting the spot at which this spring takes its rise, having joined a party assembled under the hospitable roof of one of the most opulent of the merchants of Corfu. The chateau overlooked the usual range of woodland slope, sea, and mountain. A wide stone-

balcony overhung a dark-green polished mass of
verdure, sown with the golden fruit of the orange,
and, starting from the shelving bank beneath, the
tall, white-washed belfry of a Greek chapel glared
on you, so close, that you could have almost touched
it with your hand. A fine, clear, leaping fountain broke into light close at the door, and filled
every room of the house with the sound of its cheerful gurgle, while in the garden a wilderness of
shrub and creeper hung in tangled beauty over a
succession of terraces. Good cheer, and good wine,
were succeeded by a trip in good company to the
small but well-constructed reservoir that feeds the
pipes, and so bounteous is the supply, that a lively
cascade of waste-water, hustling into its original
channel, takes flight into the vale below, rejoicing
in its liberty, and there, in a small natural-basin
fringed with wild-flowers, a group of Greek girls
were picturesquely engaged in washing clothes, as
of yore the unsophisticated daughters of King
Alcinous.

CHAPTER XIV.

On the seventeenth of May occurred one of those festas so numerous in the Greek Church. It is denominated the Feast of the Ascension, and is held on Ascension-day, on a steep rising ground called Ascension Hill, on the summit of which is a small chapel of the same name. It is one of the most popular of the year, and the whole of Corfu, either as actors or spectators, may be seen wending their way towards the spot. As the distance is less than two miles, the road is thickly strewn with pedestrians in their holiday attire, who have to keep a sharp look-out for the numerous carriages that, drawn by active little Albanian ponies, hurry to and fro at full speed, their drivers well primed in honour of the occasion with the strong black wine of Corfu. Down the hill of Castades pours the living stream, circling the bay, and on through the neat plots of the Maltese market-gardeners, then striking to the left among the hills, by villas and walled pleasure-grounds, with strips of rose-hedges and lines of aloes. Whipping and panting up a steep broken ascent, and then pulling up short under a group of olive-trees, we come to the termination of our journey and dismount.

After a few paces we emerge on the scene of action. A grove of ancient olive-trees overshadows a series of grassy knolls, which on one side overlook the sea, and of yore formed the site of the hanging gardens of King Alcinous, and in passing down their precipitous sides, the classical student may trace the wide foundations of temple and palace amid broken fragments of sculptured stone, and beside a beautiful gushing spring of water, where the remains of its former decorations lie in ruin around. Leaving antiquity to itself, let us now study the modern Greek, amid all the glory of his most famous festa.

The first conspicuous object was a street of booths, not differing widely from those seen at a country fair in England. Vendors of sugar-plums and cake, both in booths and at open stalls, plied their trade, and puffed their commodities with abundant gesticulation. Wine-sellers, sporting a small flag for a sign, presided over their store of barrels, diversified with large tins of lemonade. We soon got tired of hustling among the crowds that lounged about in this main street, as it were, of the fair, with the thermometer at eighty, and found much more to engage our curiosity in the outskirts.

On the edges of the cliffs, with their eyes turned towards the mountains of Greece, with a few thoughts perhaps of the days when the bold Epirots trod those shores in the glory of freedom and dominion, and a few hopes, perhaps, that a dawn of better days may yet arise for that land from whose fabled ones of yore they love to trace their hero-lineage, a few groups of the higher order of small proprietors sat conversing apart. The notes of a fiddle playing a very peculiar and somewhat monotonous tune, in a never-ending, still beginning measure, attracted me to a knot of spectators, and by a little dodging and standing on tiptoe, I managed to get a view of what was going on, and found myself a witness of the famous Romaic or Pyrrhic dance, the most ancient probably in the world. About twenty men, for no woman of character would be permitted to join in so public an amusement, stood in a circle, linked together by handkerchiefs, which joined the left hand of the leader to the right of him who followed next in succession, and so on to the closing dancer. Thus strung together, the only figure seemed to consist in following the leader, who conducted them round and round with a hop and step, and occasionally a vigorous caper, such as is so diverting to the spectators in the Highland fling.   Men of all ages seemed to join, and never to get tired; but what struck me most was the solemnity of the whole performance.   The vivacity of the Greek seemed to have completely deserted him.   A college Don on a hot plate could not have transferred his soles to the air with a more deadly seriousness than that with which the leader performed his allotted share of capers.   The fiddler, however, was the object that attracted my chief attention.   A thin, wiry old man, decently dressed in a plain suit of black, with grey hair floating over his shoulders, and a coal-black Greek eye, fiery with excitement, that followed every step of the dancers, and kindled with a glow of delight at every bound of more than usual agility, and flashed bitterly if a careless or weary gesture marred for a moment the spirit of the performance.   His thin, long fingers closed upon the gamut with a struggling eagerness, and the bow swept the strings with a masterly firmness, till the quaint old tune, that no doubt had often roused the revels of the henchmen of Achilles, sounded young again, as evoked by a kindred spirit, and as though it once again beat a cadence to the footsteps of heroes.   I found the same dance going on in several other places, but with no Orpheus to rival the weird old musician that had taken my fancy at first, and whose notes I could still detect as vivacious as ever.

A little retired, within the shelter of a dell, were a line of fires, piled gipsy-fashion, and over each, on a long spit made of a pole of olive wood, gyrated an animal, much resembling in size an English Jack-hare, in process of roasting. A select body of hungry Greeks looked wistfully on, and at the last turn of the spit, the cook, a stalwart Greek, lifted it from the fire, and resting the pole on end, administered a few scientific cuts to the smoking carcass, and drawing it off, it was seized from his hand by the party who had clubbed together, paid the price, and watched and inhaled the cooking of that Greek king of dishes, a lamb roasted whole. The rapidity with which the steaming delicacy is transferred, without aid of knife or fork, to the stomachs of the recipients, with not a trace left behind, except a few well-polished bones, of what had just now looked so sweet and brown, and smelt so savoury, is one of the curiosities of the festa, and many a dollar, which is the price of a lamb, is contributed by strangers for the mere purpose of seeing it accomplished. The vanished lamb is soon replaced by another, and the spit goes merrily round again, the proprietor advertising with a loud voice the treat that is in store, and a fresh set clubbing together to become purchasers. Meanwhile, a flock of these wretched innocents, folded within easy reach, and bleating piteously, are abstracted one by one, as appetite demands. A lamb thus roasted over a fire of olive-wood is pronounced by epicures to be the greatest delicacy met with in the seven islands. With exception of the dancers, the wine-bibbers, and the devourers of lamb, the majority appeared to while away their hour of enjoyment in the lazy tranquil manner so congenial to the inhabitants of the East, when unexcited. Groups squatted under the shade of the olive-trees, discussing the last news, or telling stories, rejoiced in the fragrant balm of their mild native tobacco, from within the folds of a tiny tube of silver-paper, which they prepare on the spot, as an angler does his flies, with great dexterity and neatness, (the most elegant mode, to my fancy, of inhaling the weed,) or drew it from a bowl of red Turkish clay, through a thick tube of cherry or jessamine, the end of which is pressed to the lips, a mouth-piece being invariably dispensed with. These cherry-sticks have also the reputation of being useful in the event of family differences; Pater-familias, if not greatly belied, being in the habit of using them pretty freely in cutting Gordian knots ravelled in the course of feminine disputations.

Tired at length of the heat and worry, I cau-

tiously descended the steep banks, as old Anci-
nous must have done, and zigzagging down his
hanging gardens, and picking my steps through
the prostrate fragments of his palace, I hailed a
native boat, and skimming across the quiet little
Bay of Castades, landed in less than an hour at the
foot of the citadel.

CHAPTER XV.

On the twenty-second we were reviewed by the major-general in command, who was pleased to express his approval in the following general order, dated Corfu, 24th of May 1855.

" The major-general commanding having this week inspected the R——s on parade, has much pleasure in recording his satisfaction at their steadiness under arms and correctness of manœuvres, and he does not doubt that when he inspects their quarters, books, etc., he shall find their interior economy equal to their appearance on parade."

On the twenty-fourth, being the Queen's birthday, we formed line along the castle-ramparts, and fired a " feu-de-joie" in honour of the event; and at night a grand ball was given at the palace, which was attended not only by all the military and civilians of the higher class, but by a numerous body of Greek country proprietors in their national costumes, and, in the course of the evening, the Romaic dance was performed with great eclât.

A ball at the palace of Corfu, given in the style in vogue during the administration of Sir John Young, was a sight well worth seeing, so brilliant and various were the costumes, and the rooms so well adapted to show off the spectacle to the best advantage. Entering by the principal door, you found yourself in a spacious and lofty hall, of a length nearly sufficient to permit two companies of infantry to be drawn up on each side, in front of two rows of marble pillars. Ascending a double staircase, you entered a waiting-room containing a billiard-table, the whole lighted by a large window reaching from the ground-floor to the ceiling of the second story, the light from which is moderated by a gigantic figure in bronze, in a sitting posture, on the landing-place, rather startling at the first glance, but reassuring from the civil manner in which it holds an ornamented lamp for your accommodation. Passing straight through the billiard-room, a pair of folding-doors give entrance to a neat octagon vaulted apartment, lit mainly from above, and opening at opposite sides by folding-doors on two rooms of noble dimensions and equal size, the one on the left constituting the throne-room, and that on the right a withdrawing-room. The decorations of both are elegant, but the condition of the furniture hints that the office of Lord High Commissioner is not held in permanence. In the throne-room is a life-size painting of George the Fourth in his robes of state, and in the other are two large and somewhat startling pictures representing the patron saints of the seven islands, St Michael and St George, the former badgering the devil, and the latter a dragon. Both these rooms are thrown open on grand occasions for the benefit of the dancers, the octagon serving as a haven of rest for flirtations or wall-flowers, and the billiard-hall being set apart for the band. The front of the palace, throughout its whole length, is traversed by a spacious veranda, which, protected by an awning in hot weather, forms a magnificent promenade for the dancers; the view from it on moonlight nights including, in one charming picture, the castle, the esplanade, and the city, with its tracery of lights and moving figures, while close below a fountain plays, and gigantic climbing-plants lift their offerings of flowers to the rails of the balcony.

One of the prettiest of the fêtes which occurred during our stay was the ball given by the major-general in command, at the casino or country-house of the Lord High Commissioner, at the distance of little more than a mile from the town. Standing

on the verge of a lofty line of cliffs overlooking
the Bay of Castades, whose fronts are clothed to
the very water's edge with cypresses, myrtles, and
other shrubs and creepers, is a graceful building of
white stone, Italian in style, and decorated with a
colonnade and cupola. On the three other sides of
it the ground shelves away, and is planted, park-
fashion, with an infinity of ornamental trees, a
remarkably handsome one standing apart close to
the house, grasping the ground with a trunk singularly resembling the claw of an eagle. A fruit and
flower garden, together with an orange-grove, lies
in a sheltered hollow, and out of sight, at a con-
venient distance, is a spacious kitchen-garden.

The view from it is exquisite; the mountains of
Albania, their summits sheeted in snow, but rosy
with the setting sun; the bay, castle, and city;
and, on the other side, the mingled maze of woodland and mountain that forms the glory and distinction of Corfu. Fancy this sylvan temple
delivered over to the hands of decorators and
florists, with no other orders than to compose a
fitting palace for Terpsichoré. The outside proportions were traced in bosses of Chinese lanterns.
Every room was a blaze of light from the pure
oil of the country, and every cornice, door-way,
window, and line of decorated relief, were traced
with strings of flowers in a profusion that these

climes of Flora could alone have admitted of. Three military bands, one in the interior for the use of the dancers, and two half-hidden among the evergreens at short distances, played alternately ; and at different places where a fountain could be shown to advantage, or a pretty bit of flower or foliage brought to light, invisible hands held blue lights between the pauses of the dances, and lit up the view like fairy-land.

The weather now began to betray the approach of an eastern summer, and to warn us that the active duties of drill must soon be brought to a conclusion. It was now the fourth of June, when the right wing of the regiment proceeded to a flat waste of swampy land close to the seashore, and not far from the village of Potomo, whose high slender spire showed brightly in rear of a tall white bridge in contrast with its dark woodland background. We marched from the barrack-yard at half-past four, accomplished our two-mile journey, and pitched our tents for the accommodation of men and officers, before the sun had become powerful. Targets were then erected, and the whole day spent in practising the men at ball-firing. Dinner was eaten under the tents, and the men made a gala-day of it, and, after bathing in the cool of the afternoon, returned to their barracks, having fired twenty rounds per man. The next day the ground was occupied by the left wing, and they expended our supply of practice ammunition.

The tenth of June at length arrived, the anniversary of the embodiment of the regiment, and the officers took care that, on this occasion at least, the men should have a taste of their national beverage. The dinners were prepared with extra care, and beer and bread and cheese supplied in addition. The barrack-rooms were festooned with orange, myrtle, and aloe boughs, and fifes and fiddles sustained the harmony of the evening. On the thirteenth, the sergeants gave a ball, to which all the non-commissioned officers of the garrison were invited. A large room was handsomely decorated, an excellent supper tastefully laid out, and the regimental band played its best, and kept the game up merrily till sunrise.

On the twenty-eighth, the men fell in for parade in their barrack-rooms in loose white frocks, the heat of the weather putting out-of-door drill out of the question; but they paraded for drill under the commanding-officer at five o'clock on the afternoon of Tuesday and Friday in each week.

Walking the rounds by day began now to be a serious affair between yourself and the sun. A field-officer and a captain, the former of whom took his duty by the week, and the latter by the day, had each to go either the night or day rounds, the field-officer taking his choice, with the proviso that he went three times at least at night. The officer, starting from the castle-gate, ascended the steep paths that circle the fortress, and had turned out four guards before he quitted it; then, crossing the esplanade, took his way to the new prison, a building erected on a hill about half-a-mile from the city-gates, and then returning into town, completed his rounds at a gate leading to a bathing-place, after having completed a circle of about two miles and turned out ten guards. The most important post was that which was mounted over the new prison; and I will here attempt a brief description of the building and its inmates, which, by the courtesy of the governor, I had an opportunity of inspecting. It is of modern design, and built on the radiating principle. In the centre are the apartments of the governor, who has likewise found room for a very pretty garden in which a variety of beautiful flowers are successfully cultivated.

The prisoners, in their hours of exercise, are assembled in yards, and are classified to the extent of placing together, as much as possible, those who are condemned to a like term of years. The yards are divided from each other by ranges of double cells, having each a passage in the centre into which the doors open. Each cell contains a mat and mattress for sleeping, tin utensils for eating, and

a wooden stool. Almost every man has managed
to provide himself with one or more pictures of some
Saint or scriptural subject, and some have nearly
covered their walls with specimens of their own
powers of designing. They are said to be very
constant in their devotions, and kneeling before
their small pictured shrines, apparently in earnest
prayer, appears to occupy the greater portion of
their leisure time. Working-rooms are attached
to every yard, and the trades of carpenter, tailor,
shoemaker, and straw-plaiter, flourish and abound,
and their products are in great request in the town.

The number of men condemned to imprisonment
for life exceeded, if I recollect right, fifty, of whom
no less than thirty-three were murderers, one of
whom had been guilty of no less than seventeen
separate acts of homicide; yet the conduct and disposition of this man was, in many respects, spoken
highly of by the governor. An unmanageable
temper, and the fatal habit of an instant appeal to
the knife in all matters of dispute among Greeks,
appear to have been the leading causes of his fearful catalogue of crime. As we stood by the iron
railings of the yard, the wretched herd of murderers
approached for inspection. How unfair and un-
charitable would it be to attempt to draw conclusions
and act Lavater on the countenances of these poor
wretches. Confinement, with its heart-wasting

hopelessness, the dead weight of crime on the soul, repented or unrepented, alike a consuming fiend; and all this ignominy, caged and helpless, and shown up to the passing stranger. They were not made monsters of by a suit of motley, but wore a decent habit of blue, with a cap of the same colour and material; but on one ankle a light ring of iron stamped the wearer, felon. Cain, despite his curse, was yet man, and it was surely not meet that misery like theirs should wear the garb of the buffoon. One among them I was constrained to notice and inquire of. Neither shame nor pride, nor hope nor fear, seemed known to him, as he protruded his square heavy head and coarse jaw, with shaggy eyebrows and stubby foul moustache. He had committed but two murders. He had boiled two daughters alive. One was found dead in the copper during the absence of his wife, he having been left at home in charge. It was a sad accident, and the next time the wife went abroad the neighbours watched. They were too late. He was bending quietly over the caldron, and in his right hand was a little arm, and below it seething water and the sodden corpse of his own child.

The petty rogues, denizens of the remaining yards, attracted little attention after such a magnificent show of first-class crime, with the exception of a solitary individual chipping stone in a cell. This

K

man was the sole inmate of this den of villains who
seemed all evil. So at least pronounced the governor. Neither hope, fear, indulgence, nor severity,
seemed to have power to wean him from a fierce,
unrelenting savagery that abode in him like a fiend.
As we stood near him, he worked on with a fierce
energy, as if combatting some strong resolve of
mischief that could but recoil, if indulged in, on
his own head. I was glad to move away from the
range of his evil eye, that rolled abstractedly, and
gathered light like that of an enraged animal.

There are no females in this prison. Not that the
gentle sex are altogether spotless; but their position
in this land, where oriental customs are greatly
prevalent, curtails their action both for good and
evil. There is a place of confinement within the
walls of the town for our erring sisters, and their
detention is alleviated by the good offices of a body
of nuns. There is only one other room in this
prison to which it is worth while to conduct the
reader. It is the upper story of the central tower,
from which all the buildings radiate, and contains
a large circular chapel in which are performed all
the due ceremonies of the Greek Church, and is
adorned with a handsome altar, with its adjuncts of
banner, cross, lamps, and consecrated vases. It
also forms a school in which all the unlettered
prisoners are daily assembled. In front of each

row of forms is a long narrow trough, the bottom of which is covered with a layer of fine sand. The instructor, standing on a platform, chalks on a black board a letter or numeral, at the same time naming it aloud. The prisoners in turn trace it on the sand with the tip of the finger, and proceed by gradation till they attain the power of learning from books. When the lesson is concluded, the pupil moves a sliding bar of wood along a groove in a line with the surface of the sand, and the fretted tablet becomes smooth again.

The punishment of death is a part of the law in these islands; but the repugnance of the natives to put it in force has made it almost a dead letter. The feuds engendered by civil wars and private quarrels among a barbarous people whose sole weapon consists of a knife, naturally lend a character of manslaughter to many deeds of blood which would admit of no excuse or palliation in a community as civilized as our own. A sad deed of blood was perpetrated during our stay in Corfu by a countryman of well-known evil disposition and dissolute course of life. In a fit of fury he rushed into the market-place, at a time at which it was most crowded, and stabbing a respectable lad who was standing at the door of an apothecary's shop, killed him on the spot. His next victim was a wealthy corn-broker, whom he struck in the stomach, the wound proving fatal after twenty-four hours of suffering. After an attempt at further mischief, he was fortunately pinioned from behind by a gigantic porter attached to the market, and secured. Like all villains of his kidney he commenced by boasting of his crime, lamenting his inability to destroy others that he named, and affecting mystery in regard to his motives. Then, as things approached a crisis, and the gallows loomed nearer, a small attempt at insanity and a show of penitence. In fact, he had never dreamed of a noose; but so heinous was the crime, and so much alarm had it caused among the gentry of the island, that he had to undergo the last dread preparation of passing the night, previous to his execution, in his parish church, in company with three priests, whose time is supposed to be wholly devoted to preparing him for the grave. However, the accidental absence of some one whose signature was required for the carrying out the sentence, caused sufficient delay to save his neck, and hand him over to consort with fellow-homicides for the remainder of his days. His conduct on his arrival in the gaol was on a piece with his antecedents. He boasted of high connexions, and of the interest that had been employed for him, and refused at first to obey the prison-rules like a common felon.

The prison for petty rogues is conducted on quite

another principle, and its inmates are marched out under the charge of keepers to labour on the public works, and assist in cleansing the streets. They are not accommodated with a prison-dress, and as they crowd along to their work, they give you the idea of a disarmed squad of Baschi-Bazooks who have come to grief. In the ranks of this ragged regiment there are plenty of murderers. It so happens that no convention for the mutual delivery of criminals exists between our government and that of Greece. Consequently, a subject of King Otho, who may have polished off his enemy, crosses over to the Ionian Islands, and finding work scarce, and not liking such as he finds, falls into the hands of the police, and drops down to a recruit in the Baschis.

To see this corps of Philistines at work is a sight of exquisite amusement, and many a vacant minute have I spent opposite a huge heap of limestone blocks which these creatures were set to reduce to stony batter for the construction of a new road. At least a hundred of them squatted cross-legged to their work, a hammer and a ring for testing the size of the fragment being the tools in use; and the air of listless indifference, with just a touch of curiosity, inwardly addressing it as it were, with which each contemplated his implement, and at length took it up coyly as a child does a snake, was a sight that so convulsed me with inward laughter that every hammer was suspended in mid-stroke, and a hundred strange, twinkling eyes were fixed on me at once with a ludicrous look of surprise. Something, however, must have a semblance of going on, and the *modus operandi* in fashion seemed to consist in selecting the block that sounded best when touched, and then with both eyes shut, and as much sleep as is compatible with the gentlest mechanical action of the elbow-joint, each tinkled away dolefully hammer against stone, a tuneless kind of rock-harmonicon, in the manner of a puppet-cobbler on a child's toy turned by a wheel. Sometimes, roused by the angry chatter of an over-looker, or startled by a fragment unexpectedly flying from the chosen block by dint of " *Gutta teret lapidum,*" there would suddenly open on you a wide-awake glitter of black fierce eyes and a rattling of hammers, succeeded by a proportionate lull. Hard labour in this world is no lot of theirs. May the shade of M'Adam superintend them in the next.

CHAPTER XVI.

On the nineteenth of July, the right wing of the gallant Gown and Town Regiment arrived in a sailing transport, and we welcomed that day into garrison a regiment with which we ever remained fast friends, and from whom we parted with mutual regret, and whose conduct, whether in quarters or the drill-ground, stamped them as one of the most deserving of those regiments of militia who served Her Majesty in her need at home or abroad.

On the twenty-eighth, the Royal Potteries entertained the Lord High Commissioner and the officers of the garrison to a pic-nic at a village named Beniza, about eight miles from Corfu, under the shade of some noble old olive-trees, with a back-ground of rock and mountain half-hidden in myrtle and orange trees, where a choice repast was prepared and partaken of, while, at a suitable distance, their band discoursed sweet music. Carriage after carriage followed each other and set down their load of female charms; and across the bay a tiny fleet of yachts, laden with a similar freight, raced merrily, and hove to in a bay of silver sand. As dusk advanced, quadrilles and country-dances succeeded each other in quick succession, while bonfires of dried myrtle branches in various spots lent a theatrical appearance to the scene, and contrasted well with the cool azure of the evening sky. On the twenty-fourth of the same month, our entertainers sailed for Cephalonia.

A word on pic-nics, now that we are on the subject, for here they may best be studied, tested, anatomized, and lectured on. This is their clime, their home, their cradle. No sudden shower dilutes the fragrant viands or evokes mud through the mossy carpet. No nipping gusts assail the wigs of the seniors or the crinoline of the young. The classic cicala usurps the place of the vulgar earwig, and the mantis precans does duty for the spider of our western home. You are not warned off by my lord's keeper, nor bullied by the squire's bailiff; and yet, though it may be prejudice or evil reminiscences of times gone by, I fancy an able and well-fee'd attorney might draw out a very respectable bill of indictment against three-fourths of those undertaken by roving Englishmen and maidens even in these islands of the blest. I speak not here of a well-arranged trip, where, after three hours of rapid driving through lovely and varied scenery, the white walls of the hospitable convent of Peliogestriza shine from the lofty hill that over-looks the purplest sea, and tiniest and most limpid nest of bays the sun ever made a mirror of, and set glowing like the dolphin with heaven's own tints of light and shadow. No! I shall ever call to mind, among my most pleasant reminiscences, its quaint white-washed yards, two sides bounded by the convent buildings, another by the large old chapel, and the fourth by the grotesque squat gate-way with its cross and bell, the neat cool room in which the repast was served, the rising mews of a tribe of convent cats, beseeching a dole from the depths of an outer ledge of rocks, which the windows of the hall of feasting overhung plumb down some fifty feet or more; cats, who from the convent tiles had marked the dust of the approaching carriages, and knew well the why and the wherefore and the whereabouts of the approaching feast.

Then the stroll into the old church, bowed in by the bearded priest, proud to show the array of time-honoured pictures that adorn the walls. Adam and his wife, and garden and first show of beasts, and a most reassuring delineation of the last judgment, where all their enemies were floundering in a sea of scarlet flame, wisely keeping their heads above the

surface, each head ticketed with his wicked name in
gold Greek characters like a nimbus, while far aloft
in a corner, glorified in gold and blue, their friends
looked down enjoying the scene, edified and at ease.
Then, when the fume of stale pastiles had begun
to operate tiresomely on the olfactories, a walk into
the open air, and a gossip in bad Italian with a
couple of hideous old nuns, most unromantically
employed in knitting stockings at the door of a
small building outside the convent-walls. Then a
stroll on the silver sand of the beach, or paddling
on a fisherman's raft, three-cornered and made of a
thick matting of reeds, and home at last while the
tints of dying day deepen into the darker blue of
night; and afar on the Albanian hills, now cresting
them like a coronet of fire, now wreathing round
them like a fiery serpent, or spangling them with
jets of flame, the bush-fires kindled by the Albanian
shepherds glitter " on the dusky brow of night,"
as they consume the parched refuse of the tangled
brush, to be succeeded by the sweet young grass of
next spring.

If, however, it should be imagined that a gentleman, in search of romance, can nowadays contrive
to descend, Mercury-like, on a spot all light and
shade, and wood and water, and hob-and-nob with
his Calypso in a cave of her own, all secure and
uninterrupted, he will be greatly mistaken. Sup-

pose a little pic-nic plot duly hatched, and a party
in a string of carriages, with a gay cortége of out-
riders, set out for some charming little spot, say
the Garuna pass. Everything is of the loveliest,
from the face of Nature to that of her beside you,
and the ham and pigeon-pie, with their attendant
henchmen of long-necked bottles, ride snugly below your feet in a hamper. At length the land of
promise draws nigh, and you begin to be rather
uneasy by observing that a couple of sturdy Greeks
are keeping you company on each side of the carriage, and making their presence felt by more of
your senses than one, the longer and faster you
proceed. Scouts, in the shape of ragged Greek
boys, rush frantically right and left up hills and
down ravines, bent on arousing the loose rascaldom
of the neighbouring villages to their prey. At length
the goal is gained, and a gushing spring of limpid
water, that jewel in a thirsty land, is poisoned at
its source by a herd of Greeks, who insist on forcing
their assistance on all who approach with pad or
demijohn. You dismount, and, predetermined to
have nothing to do with any of the set, bustle them
about manfully, and attain a state of fever-heat that
lasts till next morning. In the mean time the
enemy is not idle. Two Greeks are holding your
horse, and four your groom, who has resisted. You
look for help, but find that all your friends are in

an equal fix ; and, voting further resistance useless,
start for the view, or ruin, or grotto, accompanied
by the peculiar species of cortége that is wont to
escort a gang of pickpockets to the roundhouse at
a country fair. A ring is at length formed, after
the model of one prepared for a prize-fight when a
row is expected, and a sturdy set of roughs are
picked out, and bound by heavy bribes to keep the
smaller rogues at arm's length. It soon becomes
evident that the meal must be swallowed quickly.
A rencontre or two has already occurred, accompanied by a twitching of the moustache that bodes
revenge to the knife. Jeames de la Plusche has
even now been threatened with extinction, and is
trembling in all his calves from rage and fear.
Seated at length in a circle after the approved etiquette of a pic-nic, in turning round to say something soft to your fair neighbour you discover below your elbow the naked foot of a Greek boy, and
are just in time to catch a glance of him bolting
like an imp, while a silver spoon escapes through
one of the holes in his pantaloons. All soon arrive
at the conclusion that the important act of packing
up had better not be delayed, and the counting of
the silver is generally accomplished with a lugu-
brious face. The last scene of all, that ends this
strange eventful history, is the payment of the con-
stables. First the ladies and old men are hurried

away and made secure in the carriages, and then at the sight of the coins comes a rush such as won Marathon. Rogues and roughs are indiscriminately mingled, and as they all implore, threaten, and protest in the same breath, and all chatter, smell, and look as like one another as rotten eggs, it ends in something very like a scramble, in the midst of which the strong-minded individual who has undertaken the post of paymaster seeks safety in flight, like the man who withdraws the bar of the pit-door on a boxing night.

It is now my task to relate a tragic event, which excited a painful excitement among the men, and threatened to bear evil fruit for the future. I was enjoying myself at a ball which our hospitable major was in the habit of giving every fortnight during the summer season, when news was brought that one of my company had been just carried to the hospital in a dying state from the stab of a knife. I hurried to his bedside, and found one of the finest of my men lying in an exhausted state, but perfectly sensible. From what I could gather from his own statement, and from that of a comrade who was near him at the time, it seemed that while on his way to the barracks for tattoo, and within a score or two of yards from the gate, he was suddenly stabbed in the groin, while the assassin disappeared across the esplanade so quickly that not a trace of him could be discovered. On the side of the poor fellow's white trousers, now soaked in blood, a clean-cut incision, not half an inch in length, marked the passage of the deadly knife. Very small was the outward appearance of the wound, and the doctors could give no decided opinion on his chance of life. In this sad state of suspense the poor man lingered for about twenty-four hours, and then died suddenly and unexpectedly without a struggle. An inquest, consisting of a field-officer and two captains, recorded a verdict of wilful murder; and suspicion was excited against a Greek hawker, who had often been busy about the barracks, and with whom the murdered man had been on bad terms on account of some transaction relative to the sale of a watch. The officers of the regiment lost no time in offering a reward of fifty pounds, to which Sir John Young, on the behalf of government, added fifty more, and so anxious were the townspeople to testify the sense of the good conduct of the men, that they increased the reward to one hundred and fifty pounds, and handbills were posted throughout the town, in Greek, Italian, and English, to advertise the fact.

In addition to the huckster already in custody, evidence was brought forward implicating another Greek, with whom the murdered man was known to have had a quarrel. However, after a series of examinations, which occupied four months, it was found impossible to fix the deed on either of the accused. On the evening of the sixth, the funeral procession wended its slow way through the sunny roads of the esplanade. The whole regiment followed, with the band at the head, playing the Dead March in Saul. The procession soon reached the little square burial-ground, with its Iytch gate surmounted with a cross. It is situated on an angle of the outworks, and is secured by strong iron gates and lofty walls, whose summits are serried with broken glass, so difficult is it to prevent religious rancour from defacing the tomb and filching any saleable ornament from the grave of a heretic.

The sensation created by this assassination was greatly stimulated among the lower orders by the determination of the Greek clergy to excommunicate publicly the unknown perpetrator. The jealousy with which the garrison of a foreign nation is naturally regarded by the populace was imbittered at this time by the events of the war, the Greeks espousing with intense enthusiasm the cause of their co-religionists the Russians, and regarding with proportionate disgust the presence and control of their antagonists. With them a soldier dead was simply a soldier the less, and why should any questions be asked, especially such as might become troublesome? It was in order to counteract as much as possible such sentiments as these, that the priests, to whom their flocks look with the respect and awe exacted by a church militant amid a host of foes, determined on so solemn a ceremony. The archbishop, a man whose character and attainments were acknowledged by men of all ranks and parties, is said to have been the first to have proposed it. Accordingly, on the day-week succeeding the crime, an unusual concourse might have been observed on the esplanade, gathering in groups and conversing moodily, and at five o'clock a procession was seen wending its way at funeral-pace from the church of St Spiridion. The outer robes of the priests were black, and in front was carried a massive cross of the same sombre hue. Priests and acolytes also bore in their hands lighted tapers of black wax. They took up a position in a circle within an open space kept clear for them by the police. The crowd, bareheaded and silent, looked on with an awestruck expression; but the chief objects of attraction were the two suspected prisoners, who, in custody of the police, were brought from durance to witness the ceremony. They were much alike in size and height, but one had the short, black, close-curled hair which is more characteristic of the Maltese than the Greek, and a pair of dark coarse whiskers, contrasting strongly with his ashen pale face; but the eye was calm and steady, and his attitude singularly free from nervousness or defiance. The other had comparatively light hair, with thin compressed lips and scanty moustache, and a cunning but not altogether evil expression. He was not quite so much at his ease as his companion, but his eye and gestures betokened rather curiosity than fear. The priests, the majority of whom were aged men, then proceeded to chant a service, which I have no doubt resembled to some extent our commination service, and at a particular part of it the lights were suddenly extinguished by reversing the tapers. A hoary priest, " whose beard descending swept his aged breast," next stepped into the centre of the circle, and, lifting his hand toward the sky, poured forth a diatribe against the crime with impassioned words and animated gestures. The procession then re-formed, and returned silently to the church, the populace dispersing slowly and sullenly, but evidently impressed by what they had seen and heard.

The number of priests resident in Corfu bears a very large proportion to the population, but the chapels are so thickly scattered both in town and country, that surprise on that score ceases, only to be renewed on the subject of whence come the funds derived for their support; but a little inquiry succeeds on throwing light on it. As you watch their tall dark figures moving statelily along, the upright

L

peakless cap displaying the full expanse of forehead, while the ample silky beard, silver-white or raven, depends grandly on their chests, the straight delicately chiselled Grecian nose, and eyes of liquid black so peculiar to the race, the figure enlarged both in height and amplitude by the dark flowing drapery of their robes; you will be obliged to confess, not only that they are specimens of an eminently handsome race, but that they partake every inch of them of the dignity of a selected priesthood.

Not that exceptions do not frequently occur. The weak and the ill-favoured are not altogether excluded, and in the weather-beaten plebeian face, and patched and grimy apparel of the majority of those who trudge in from the neighbouring villages, are seen unmistakable signs of poverty. Some of these latter carry small brass boxes, with a slit in the lid, into which the faithful are expected to contribute an offering in assistance of their chapels. In fact, a large proportion of the Greek clergy are, both in birth and habits, little above the race of peasantry, and after being provided with the habiliments of a priest, which cover a multitude of sins in trousers, shirts, and stockings (very few priests show well in a high wind), they support their dignity on bread and sardines, and rear their family in a little loft over their chapel, or hovel adjoining it, and often in a portion set apart from the chapel itself, from whose upper windows the comely Mrs Priest, with her little flock, may frequently be seen chatting with a passing friend, while the sonorous chant of her husband, pealing through his good-looking nose in the chapel below, proclaims the glad earnest of an uninterrupted gossip, in which any abuse of himself will be drowned in his own music. Indeed, I have reason to think, that, where the profane are few and the room cosy, a little domestic bliss will penetrate the sanctum ; for, once stepping into a remote chapel, I discovered on a small table before the Virgin and Child, and within an inch of her votive lamp, a pair of scissors, a ball of wax, a skein of thread, and a bit of riband.

Having made mention of the English cemetery, I will here attempt a short description of the Greek one. It lies at the distance of rather more than a mile from the city, on the road that leads through the village of Castades, and lies a few hundred yards from the high road. A row of cypresses skirts either side of the approach, with a neat porter's lodge, and a pretty spring of water opposite, which drips from a rock shaded with ferns and flowers, and is collected in a primitive basin formed of a barrel sunk into the ground. The path continues a short way farther, and you then arrive at a large iron gate, whose only distinction is a large ornamental Greek cross. Entering through this, you find yourself in a square space of ground, containing about six acres, on the declivity of an inclined plane, which is rendered more level by being divided into two portions by means of a terrace, to which you gain access by a flight of steps. On this terrace stands the chapel, a large white building, with a portico in front and two small aisles on each side. The ground is surrounded by plain walls of inconsiderable height, and is laid out in straight walks on a very simple plan, while the graves are ranged on each side, with a view to the economy of space. Nearly every grave is marked by a small wooden cross painted black, and on many of them are suspended garlands and nosegays. Not a few are enclosed by a light iron railing, with a little wilderness of rose and geranium in the centre.

On mounting the terrace, it becomes evident that you are treading the floor of a sort of upper house of departed worthies. Tombs of pretension, heavy enough to make the poor occupant below aware of the pressure of the honours done him, and coats of arms, and arms and orders once on coats, sculptured over a list of titles, tell their last tale of human vanity. There are a few groups in alto relievo, but of small artistic merit, and the chief peculiarity is their position over the tomb, on which they rest slanting like a picture on an easel. The interior of the chapel differs little from that of others.

It is simply a high room with oaken stalls on each side, and paintings of the Virgin and Child, with .saints and angels, swarthy and gilded, are rejoicing in an atmosphere of pastiles. A bier and pall lie on one side, ready for use.

While I was there, a man accompanied by two friends arrived, carrying under his arm a little pink coffin, while one of his companions followed with the lid. Within it, smothered in flowers, was the corpse of a little child, and as all previous ceremonies had been performed in the parish church, the body was conveyed at once into one of the side aisles appropriated to that purpose. The father then kissed the corpse with much emotion, and after praying over it withdrew. Beside it on the same ledge lay another tiny pink coffin, with the pallid face of a chubby boy peering through the flowers. The lids of both coffins were placed upright beside them, and it is customary for the bodies to remain there during the night, and the next day they are interred without further ceremony. On another occasion, as I was strolling down the lower walk, I observed two men shabbily dressed baling the water from out of an open grave, and near them an aged priest superintending the work. A black coffin, with a cross marked in white calico along the whole length of the lid, lay close by. As I looked on with some curiosity, the old priest signed to the men to remove the lid, which was only secured by a single tack, and there lay the body of an elderly woman, decently clothed in a black stuff gown, with white stockings, and a kind of turban of the same colour, and a band beneath the jaw. She lay in an easy position, with the face somewhat turned aside, and the arms decently but negligently reclining beside her. The earth of this cemetery is reported to possess the property of preventing the decay of the human body, a peculiarity which does not enhance its value in the eyes of the Greeks, among whom there exists a strong prejudice in favour of the early decomposition of the dead.

There is one other place of burial, over which I have frequently trodden with a strange sense of interest. On a shelving slope, which once formed part of the glacis of a portion of the outer fortifications, an uneven surface of stony soil, with scarce a weed to impart a speck of foil to its universal barrenness, descends to one of the public roads. Across it, as a short cut, cows, sheep, goats, and donkeys are constantly on the move, or make it their temporary lair, and the wear and tear of their hoofs, and their filth and litter, add a look of squalor to the desolate view. Yet thick as leaves in Vallombrosa are scattered a layer of slabs, on whose surface, surrounded with quaint emblems and mystic signs, are carved the letters that Moses read on the tablets direct from the Almighty. Here is the Ghetto of the dead. Here the body of the despised Jew returns to a dust as flinty as that of Shylock, if it corresponds to that within which it is entombed.

Let us now turn to a livelier theme, and pass to the interior of the handsome temple in which the descendants of Thespis hold their court. Their court here, however, is anything but that of a despotic monarch. To the throne of tinsel is chained a remorseless fate, whose modern designation is " The Opera Committee;" and grave and solemn, sedate and charged with destiny, Rhadamanthus-like, in stage jury-box, does this committee hold its sitting, when for the first night the curtain rises and exhibits the heroes and heroines of a four months' season. On the thirteenth of September, at eight P. M. by the clock, commenced the fearful trial. Mailed knights and noble dames swept over the stage, which was their dock. The foot-lights seemed to glare upon them, and to shed on the eyes of that awful conclave in the committee-box a lurid light, which they alone could bear serene and unwinking. The first act was over. The promiscuous and somewhat ragamuffin lot that discoursed music, such as it was, in the orchestra, had re-rosined their bows with a smirk, and watered the floor from their twisted tubes. Again the mimic scene was displayed. Again the voice of the mailed warrior pealed in baritone, to be answered by his rival in buckram and basso, while the princess domineered in treble; and so high grew the melée that no less a person than the Emperor Frederick Barbarossa himself was obliged to come to the rescue, with his mouth ready in a circle; when, to that monarch's extreme disgust, without giving him time for a note, bass, tenor, or baritone, at a signal from the bar of Rhadamanthus, down thundered the curtain like a guillotine, and cut short the head and front of all their offendings.

Let us turn now from the mimic scene of love, war, and murder, to a spot whereon a meaningless farce of tragico-buffoonery is carried on, without hindrance of time or season, on a tight little island that lifts its back out of the bay about two miles from shore. The stage on which the actors fret, in spite of themselves, far longer than the hour allotted by Shakspeare, is enclosed within an oblong square of worm-eaten buildings. The flag that waves in front has not a gala look, though it is of a flaunting yellow, yet here are borne by resistless fate, in the shape of a Sanatá officer, in boat, barge, and steamer, the young, the old, the rich and poor, the gentle and simple. All alike look dolorous and draggle-tailed, and some glare savagely. The highly principled affect the calm of undeserved injury. The more vulgar herd would be more clamorous if they dared, and swear under their breath in a polyglot of languages. Each individual, as he is shovelled ashore, is conducted through a latticed door, and within the area of the building is shown into a den in which it is his fate to lie and be cleansed. A bearded policeman does duty as domestic, and is supposed to dress the hair of the ladies and arrange their crinoline. A table and a chair or two are presumed to possess in this place most wonderful powers of adaptation, and to assume the properties of mattress, bed, mirror, and every other article of domestic necessity, such as in our duller climes is only to be witnessed in pantomimes. Just as a wretch begins to be so excessively foul and mildewed as to feel only fit to shun his kind, he is turned over to society as clean, and, on paying his bill, may depart.

Now a word on the crime which entails so fearful a punishment. Suppose in London or Liverpool, or the ports of France and the Adriatic, sundry old women should experience the pains and penalties of a more than usually expressive colic; straightway, on the wings of the lightning-wire, runs the sad tale of the symptoms, and as it is most reasonable to suppose that passengers arriving from such ports have either seen, heard, touched, or smelt the said old women, and are thereby rendered dangerous to a society that feels itself sound beneath the girdle, so it follows that the said new arrivals are bound to be made to feel from what a foul spot they must last have emanated, and to what a haven of cleanliness, even to prudery, they have arrived. To prevent the game getting slow and keep the sulphur caldron simmering, a large preserve of barren breezy highlands and tangled copse, in which the wild boar has his lair, and the very genius of health, freedom, and exercise might be supposed to fix on as his chosen home, has been selected and set apart as anathema and irreclaimable from disease; and the sportsman daring enough to set foot on the mountain fastnesses of Albania must be accompanied, at his own expense, by a policeman whose duty is to prevent his coming in contact with man, woman, or child, cloth, leather, or wool, and a legion other such enormities, which otherwise would, on his return, worthily consign him to the *peine forte et dure* of confinement and trial by sulphur.

Do not suppose that these indignities are confined to those that breathe the breath of life. That spasms should travel in a letter is quite in accordance with common sense, so pray inform the gentle Anna Matilda not to be rash enough to enclose her lovely portrait in your next expected, or it will arrive starred with the stabs of a cruel piece of cutlery, and carry with it a scent as though straight from the regions of purgatory; and caution your affectionate mamma and sister to refrain sending by post those turquoise studs they bought for you at Paris, as studs can't be worn when smashed to fragments, as a comrade of mine knows well to his cost. Never did our brave regiment smell so deeply of villanous saltpetre as on the days that brought the heavy mail, Her Majesty's letter-bag being perfumed like a hayrick that has been on fire.

One fine day, however, down came the dreaded cholera spite of all precautions. How he got ashore became a puzzle to all right-minded people. Was he thrown overboard in a bottle, or did he survive his dose of sulphur from its want of strength or other fatality. The profane hinted that insufficient diet, drains open and drains choked, and no drains at all where drains ought to abound, and hovels foul and reeking, and lanes in which the foot of scavenger never trod, were the very garnish of his chosen home, so that he might possibly have been born here, a native in fact. At any rate, he grew big here and prospered, and had a commission named to attend him, and a staff of doctors to swell his pride, and a graveyard of his own on an old bastion a nice mile out of town, where, on their arrival, with scant ceremony and few mourners, he kept his victims under his own eye. In the meantime, to do them justice, never did the sanatory authorities wage fiercer war at the outposts than when their adversary had securely intrenched himself in the citadel. Never did the oars of the sanita boat lash the water more viciously at the luckless approaching vessel; never was more sulphur or saltpetre set smoking; never was suspected wight in grimmer durance. A certain small village in Cumberland is famous for an attempt on the part of its inhabitants to hedge in the cuckoo, and thereby secure a perpetual spring. They met with no success; but they were a handful of rustics. The game of hedging out the cuckoo is played here on a much grander scale, and if the process is not altogether a sweet one, it is dignified with seals of office, autographs of the high and mighty, banners, barges, and black-mail. For my own part, I never had any personal quarrel with the health department, except for their having, of *malice prepense*, placed at the head of it as kind-hearted a veteran as ever bore Her Majesty's commission. I hope and pray they may send him home with a noble pension and time to repent. The officers of the quarantine island were also, as far as in them lay, civil and obliging.

The cholera mercifully spared the Royal Blanks, not a single case of it having been admitted into our hospital; but on the seventeenth of October, a large transport came into port, having on board the Royal Parkshire Regiment, who disembarked the same afternoon, and took up their quarters in Fort Neuf. On them the fell disease seized with a strange malignity, and, day after day, the muffled drums of that unfortunate corps resounded along the avenues of the esplanade, until orders were issued that in future the funerals should be unaccompanied by music, the unusual frequency of the dead march being judged likely to produce a feeling of despondency in the survivors. A change of quarters to the healthy little island of Vido was next tried, but without much immediate success, and it became necessary to form there a small graveyard for the accommodation of this unfortunate regiment, and in a sheltered little hollow, surrounded by shelving banks of luxurious vegetation and bushes of myrtle and acanthus, I counted twenty-three mounds, marking the last resting-places of these poor fellows.

On the twenty-first of October, No. One company of our regiment sailed for the classic island of Ithaca, but there not being sufficient accommodation on board her, either as regards stores or quarters, the Ulysses of the day refused them permission to land, and, after enduring much hardship from crowded decks and scant supply of water, they disembarked again at Corfu on the afternoon of the twenty-third. As this unlucky voyage was the origin of much future official correspondence, I will leave the gallant commander of that ill-starred expedition to relate his own story as set forth in his official report.

"*Ionian Steamer, 23d October* 1855.

"MY LORD,—I have the honour to inform you, that on the Ionian steamer arriving at Ithaca, I found there was not the slightest accommodation for the troops on board. There were only four tents in the storekeeper's hands, a very small quantity of salt provisions in store, and the contractor had only fresh provisions for fifty men for twenty days. Now, considering we had five officers, one hundred and ninety-six men, fifteen women, and twenty-two children on board, besides the crew, it was impossible to undergo quarantine under such circumstances at Ithaca. I therefore, as commanding-officer on board, ordered the steamer to proceed to Cephalonia, where I expected, from what I was told by those in authority in Ithaca, to find every accommodation; but such was not the case. Colonel Talbot very kindly did all he could for us in the way of provisions, as we were obliged to throw away the greater part of the two days' rations served out to the men in Corfu, as they were not fit to eat.

"Colonel Talbot could not take us into the

lazaretto or the quarantine island, both of these places being occupied. He therefore gavé us orders, as soon as I had got the provisions on board, to return to Corfu directly, which I have done, but not without great difficulty and danger. —I have the honour, &c.

" B. R."

About this time the weather began to grow cooler, and the men resumed the coatee and chaco. On the thirtieth, the opera opened once more with a fresh company, and the Traviata of Verdi was successfully performed, and the season continued without interruption till the beginning of Lent.

I must here stop to mention, that all the rank and file of warriors that trod the boards of the stage were selected from the Royal Blanks, and whether standing sentry over a dungeon, apprehending a ruffian, escorting a princess, or quelling a revolution, they invariably behaved in a manner to reflect the highest credit on the corps.

On the thirty-first, the garrison received a strong reinforcement by the arrival of the Royal Metropolitan Rangers, a very strong and efficient regiment; but it was not destined for us to remain long as close neighbours, without experiencing a few of those little sallies of contempt which familiarity is said to be so industrious in breeding.

Why or wherefore, in these days of free trade, when foreign hams and flitches encumber the hooks of the city chandler, the chawing of bacon should still be regarded as an attribute solely appertaining to the genus bumpkin;—why or wherefore the imputation of the aforesaid "chawing" should in turn be so indignantly rejected by the agricultural mind, is an enigma, the solution of which I must leave to abler philosophers; but it is true, alas! that from these porcine jests were farrowed a noisy litter of petty squabbles that came to a crisis on the afternoon of Sunday the sixteenth of December, frighted the citizens from their propriety, contributed not a little practice to the surgeons, set all the officers at their wits' end, brought its usual complement of pickets and precautions, caused a court of inquiry that sat a month and elicited nothing but a little bad language, a speech from the commanding-officer, and an order from the general; which at last, I am happy to say, was all followed by a reconciliation between the regiments, which lasted till our departure from the island.

About this time I took an opportunity of going on board a Swedish frigate that had paid the harbour a visit. I found the officers all spoke English fluently, and I was most kindly received on board. Everything appeared very clean and ship-shape.

The small-arms on board all loaded at the breech; a plan, which I was informed by the captain, had been in use for the last six years in the Swedish army, and was found to answer well. I was much amused with the marine on sentry, who was a merry little Swede, with a head so flat, that it was a puzzle to understand how his big heavy helmet held on to such a plane surface. His blue uniform was peppered with a light coating of fluff, as though he had been recently tossed in a blanket. Pipe-clay and he were not friends, as his belt proclaimed aloud, and his sword adhered peacefully to its scabbard. The ammunition in his pouch consisted of two crusts of black bread and a roll of tobacco. When he presented arms he accompanied the motion with a kind of whoop. Altogether, he personified a kind of composite emblem of peace and war.

The weather now began to break up, and a succession of heavy thunder-storms deluged the streets. The booming of the thunder among the mountains of Albania, and the flashes that seemed to sear their sides, and light up the foamy billows of the Mediterranean at their feet, was grand beyond description, and has kept me many a night on the balcony watching the dark and troubled waste before me. Cold bitter winds prevail by fits and starts at this season, and they taught me the fact, that the most miserable dog beneath the moon is a cold Greek. Wrapped in their capotes of goat or sheep skin, they crawl shivering along, with scarce enough of life left to keep their roguery warm; or, on the sides of the roads, involved in their coverings like a caterpillar in his husk, lie motionless, and give one the idea of a dead animal.

On the third of this month, the major-general inspected narrowly the regimental books, barrack-rooms, and interior economy of the regiment, and on the twenty-seventh, a long and successful field-day took place before him, and the next day the following order appeared in the regimental books, and closed the achievements of the Royal Blanks for the year 1855.

" REGIMENTAL ORDERS.
" *Corfu*, 28*th December* 1855.

" The lieutenant-colonel congratulates the officers, non-commissioned officers, and men, on the appearance of the regiment in the field before the major-general yesterday. It was most satisfactory, and shows that all have strenuously exerted themselves to maintain the high character the regiment has hitherto enjoyed.

" The major-general expressed himself in language most complimentary to the regiment, as to its efficiency in the field, and the cleanliness and regularity of the barrack-rooms. The lieutenant-colonel feels certain that the men under his command will exert themselves to the utmost to preserve the good name they now have, and which is the source of so much gratification to him and all the officers of the R ————."

CHAPTER XVII.

A. D. fifty-six opened merrily on the officers of the garrison of Corfu. The good old strain of " Auld lang syne" soothed the dying ear of fifty-five, and the brisk and modern melody, " There's a good time coming," gladdened the cradle of fifty-six. The place where the revel was held was again the Casino, where an officer of the Parkshire gave us a first-rate ball, and young fifty-six had opened his eyes pretty widely before the majority of the assembled guests had retired to shut theirs.

On the fourth, the noble line-of-battle ship the St Jean d'Acre, 101 guns, steamed into port, and was followed, on the sixth, by the Hannibal, 91, bearing the flag of the Admiral Sir Houston Stewart. On the ninth, the naval officers gave a grand dejeuné, on board the St Jean d'Acre, to the Lord High Commissioner, the garrison, and civilians,

and, after an excellent luncheon, a dance was got
up on the quarter-deck, which was profusely ornamented with flags and evergreens. The company
separated but to meet again at the palace, where a
grand ball concluded the day's work, and the
rooms were crowded with the uniforms of the two
services. Ladies were in the request they desired
and deserved, but those approaching the designation of fat, fair, and forty, were invariably mono-
polized by the middies. Nor was all the enjoyment confined to the magnificos. Shoals of eman-
cipated tars, rushing up the beach like young
water-lions, scoured every alley of Corfu, and from
the highest, "the lowest, the loneliest spots," evoked
sounds of laughter, terror, and jollity. Bacchus
quite dispossessed St Spiro for that week at least,
who, had he attempted his circuit through his
peculiar streets, would, most probably, have been
compelled to go aboard, or have had a ride more
like a Guy than a Saint. They patronized the
opera, and half a regiment had to be despatched to
keep the doors from being torn down, for the
Greeks, outstripping all recognised rules of roguery,
had sold them bits of card-board at ten shillings a
head, by way of tickets, and one man had given a
sovereign for the knave of clubs. The pit that
night was all humour and jollity, and the actors
received such complimentary personalities, that

they could not keep their countenances, while the boxes were filled with an audience whose attraction was the pit. The baritone, a plump heavy man, in a grand costume, had just got his mouth open during a moment of dead silence, when a loud earnest voice broke out with, " My eyes, what a good-looking gentleman !" and he was obliged to shut it again incontinently in consequence, and could hardly get through his part. All the proceedings were marked with great good humour, and really redounded much to the credit of the service. If rum flowed a little too freely, it was, at all events, equally shared, and the finer parts of the singing were listened to with great attention.

This siege of Corfu lasted about three days, and never could a better harvest have been reaped by the knavery of the lower Greeks. A festa happening to fall at the same period, the shops were shut, and Jack thereby prevented from showing off so many of his usual freaks, but curs and birds were bought at fabulous prices. One man bought a donkey, and after riding in triumph about the esplanade till he was sore, made it a new-year's gift to the first man he chanced to speak to. A five-pound note was eaten by another between bread and butter, and a carriage-load of tars, each with a broom held aloft, galloped up and down the esplanade. At Malta, the first act of a frigate's crew on the spree had been to provide each man with a white hat and a pair of blue spectacles. Opposite my house was a large fountain, close to the fountain one of those quaint little old chapels, so numerous and nondescript, and in the loft of this old chapel a more than usually dirty old priest, a cat, a hen, and a full-grown brood of ducks. The old priest was accustomed, at the matin-hour, to escort these said ducks to the fountain for an hour's recreation, regarding them with all the pride of property as they cut their watery gambols. One morning, hearing more noise than usual, I looked out of window, and found that the group had been joined by a troop of Hannibals, who were just rollicking back to their ship. In a moment every sailor had his duck, while the poor old priest, in a frenzy of anxiety and terror, was spun like a teetotum within a circle of admiring tars, his long grey beard and tatterdemalion dressing-gown creating intense amusement. At length, after he had passed through an ordeal similar to that of pantaloon at the Adelphi, his scattered brood were collected for him, and he retired to his loft, to pray doubtless for any wind that would clear the bay of men-of-war. On the tenth, the two ships got up steam, and steered for Malta.

At this season the garrison commenced marching out into the country, in order to accustom the men to carry their packs, and become efficient for taking the field, if necessary, in their new climate. Each regiment had a different route assigned to it, and the distance to be traversed was four miles, when the men were halted, the arms piled, the packs taken off, and deposited according to rule in a line with the arms, and then pickets were thrown forward, and sentries posted on the heights, and in such order as to keep the main body from any danger of surprise. After a halt of three-quarters of an hour, the pickets were recalled by sound of bugle, and the men returned to barracks. These little promenades, which occurred twice a-week, were, no doubt, of great use to the men. Exercise, change of air and scene, and escape from the stale monotony of the parade-ground, set them all in spirits, and the welcome halts under the shade of olive-trees were generally scenes of fun and frolic.

The officers frequently set the men scrambling for oranges, and then there were lizard and snake-hunts, and the naturalists, armed with knives, hunted out and extracted the curious dormitories of the trap-door sider. This funny, fat, black-looking fellow, makes himself a home in the bottom of a pipe, from six to ten inches deep, buried in a bank, about the size of the interior of a flute, and softly lined with a substance resembling silver-paper. On the top is a kind of button fastened with a hinge of silk, which closes firmly after being lifted. The exterior of this button is made to correspond precisely with the spot on which it lies, be it moss, bark, or lichen, and it requires a keen eye to detect the cheat.

On one of our lines of march, a short distance from the town, we used to pass the site of a Roman burial-ground, which had been lately discovered. The coffins lay very thick, and were of immense size, roughly chiselled, but in workmanlike style, and were without lids. Many were square, or nearly so, and exactly resembled the stone tanks used for rain-water in town-houses in England, and some were even large enough to contain from ten to twenty bodies. They were now being dug up by the peasantry and sold for water-troughs.

On the sixteenth of January, our mess-room was adorned with all the art the decorative genius of the regiment was able to muster,—crowns, flags, and stars of swords and bayonets, bright with the reflected rays of numerous lamps; and there was the usual overflow of flowers and evergreens, and the band played their best for the honour of the corps till daylight did appear. This ball was given by the lieutenant-colonel, and on the thirtieth, the scene was renewed by the officers, who in turn lent a hand to keep the belles of Corfu from their pillows; and, on the fourth of February, a grand garrison-ball took place in a large building called the College, which had originally been a barrack, but appropriated latterly as a school for Greek youths. The library, a large square room, was allotted to the dancers, and so prettily draped with a screen of white and coloured calico, richly relieved with flags and flowers, that the original destination of the place could never have been guessed at by the sharpest observer. As night wore on, however, and the footfalls of the dancers assaulted the floor, on which the grave heavy thump of the professor's foot was alone wont to break silence, the neglected tomes began secretly and surely to avenge themselves for the contempt they endured, and the flippant impudence which had hidden their solemn faces with a screen so indecorous; and gave out such a cloud of learned dust, that eyes, nose, and mouth, partook of their classic lore. The fondest flirtation frequently ended in a sneeze. The rose the enraptured lover had borne off in triumph turned out little sweeter than a snuff-box, and the last glance of the eyes of beauty electrified him with a wink.

The grand ball of the season was a fancy-dress one, given at the palace on the twenty-fourth of January. Then were the fingers of tailors and seamstresses on the alert, from the artistes of Paris,

who held high converse on frill and flounce by aid
of the electric telegraph, to the dingy Judiths who
slaved for the opera-costumier in the slums of the
Jews' quarter. Eight gentlemen in the rich mous-
quetaire dress of the time of Louis Quatorze, led
off the ball with a minuet d'amour, their partners
being in costly and elegant costumes of the same
period, and each couple matched in colour. Then
a set of lancers, by Zouaves and Vivandières, and
another of the officers of the Guards of the reign of
George the Second, with partners in court-dresses
of the same period. The usual crowd of Turks,
Sailors, and Circassians, down to a navvy from the
Crimea, joined in the melée, and polked, galloped,
and quadrilled, till daylight.

This is the carnival season at Corfu, and it is
finished off by a grand masked-ball at the theatre.
Of the carnival I can say but little. It lasts above
three weeks, and is represented at first by two or
three very dirty disguises made up of blankets and
shawls, and gaudy handkerchiefs, which, I should
think, must make the wearers intolerably hot,
especially as they are generally the centre of a
crowd, and, at times, find it necessary to skip
about nimbly. As the days advance, the number
of masks multiply considerably, a few attempts
are made at assuming characters, and a few car-

riages filled with masks drive up and down the esplanade. The astonishment and curiosity of the soldiers at first knew no bounds, but an order having come out that the masks were in no way to be interrupted, it was strictly obeyed, and no act of discourtesy occurred during the whole time.

The carnival-ball was held in the theatre, and commenced at nine o'clock; but, with the exception of a very few cases, no attempt was made at supporting characters, and, after watching for an hour or so, the novel effect of some three or four hundred of both sexes in nondescript dresses, whirling and leaping to the sound of music, the majority of the occupants of the boxes retired. A portion of the court-party were among the spectators, and a few masks visited the boxes and mystified their occupants.

A child's fête, given in the palace by Lady Young, gave more pleasure to many of us than the grander balls, of which by this time we were all well-nigh tired. The throne, with the sword of state lying across it, was soon assailed and taken possession of. A handsome child, with a little girl on his left hand, assumed the royal seat with the greatest gravity, but were assailed by a host of little rebels, who looked all the more formidable from having hunted out and assumed the swords and caps of their seniors, which had been laid aside. The crimson steps of the throne "were covered with a bevy of gaily dressed imps, restless as ants, many in a topsy-turvy predicament, and all agog for fun and mischief.

CHAPTER XVIII.

ABOUT this time a tour of duty caused my departure to the island of Cephalonia. I embarked in a
gale of wind at four P. M. on board one of the
Austrian line of packets, at five next morning we
came to anchor off the town of Argostoli, and in a
few minutes I found myself in an open boat, pulling ashore. It required no lengthened observation
for the eye to embrace the scene that now presented
itself. We were enclosed in a winding creek, shut
in on both sides by lofty hills of singular and for-
bidding barrenness. At the foot of those, on the
right, a natural plateau gave room for the white
buildings and tall steeples of a considerable town,
which seemed to hug the water's edge, and throw
out a succession of piers like arms, stealing forward,
as it were, into the domains of the sea, in the
struggle to escape from the barrenness in the rear.

Behind the town, and high above it, a few desperate olive-bushes clung to the stony ribs of the rock, brindling them with dusky specks, and on their summit, which was of smaller extent and elevation than those on the opposite shore, was a signal-station of very unpretending dimensions. Following the rugged profile of the shores, the eye was arrested by a something that cut the water-line in an abrupt streak, lying on the surface, and beyond it was a show of green that told of vegetation.

On landing, we entered on a broad road lying between the water and the first line of houses, except where it was encroached upon by a large building or two, used apparently as storehouses, and partially built on piles. I soon entered the interior of the town, and found the streets were numerous, and many of respectable width, and adorned with several quaint old houses and handsome clean chapels. The shops were not yet open; but I afterwards discovered that there were certain of them superior, in some respects, to any in the seven islands, and that Queen Corfu herself sometimes finds it to her advantage to do her shopping here—so at least affirm the residents. The only reason I could discover for this appeared to be, that in consequence of its large exports of currants and tobacco, this island has more direct dealings with England than her more famous sister. During my

stay on board the packet, I had made the acquaintance of a Greek Count, who was on his return from
London, where he had left his Countess, in order to
overlook his property, and see that the requisite
farming operations for the next vintage of wine, oil,
and currants, were in course of being attended to.
He was enthusiastic in his praise of English hospitality, and, in return, requested me and an officer
who accompanied me, to use his house as long as
we had occasion to stay in the island, and at once.

He led the way to a large postern-door, which
gave entrance to a small court-yard, and ascending
a flight of stone steps, we found ourselves in the interior of a curious and very extensive old mansion,
strange-shaped and rambling, and guiltless of paint
or plaster, the chief material of its internal construction being wood, which length of time had
stained and warped, and yet it was impossible not
to acknowledge a something interesting in its large
panelled walls, and multifarious chambers, decorated with French sporting-prints of a bygone
period, with here and there an antique cabinet and
bit of ancient sculpture. In one room a large collection of paintings, ancient and modern, were
piled without order on the floor, and in a small
kind of closet, a collection of pictured saints, black
with age, and in carved worm-eaten frames, surrounded an old wooden cross; into this sanctum

the family-priest comes twice a-week, and performs prayers on behalf of the family. A cup of hot coffee, and the wherewithal to perform the duties of the toilet, was the extent to which we found it necessary to trench on his hospitality; but, on a future visit, he drew from the recesses of his cellar some specimens of wine from his own vineyard, of great age, and very delicate flavour. To add to its rarity, it was served in old Venetian glasses ornamented with gold. As a relish he produced the roe of a fish pressed to a hard mass, and prepared by some peculiar process. The flavour was very strong and relishing, but remained so long on the tongue, that I declined a second slice of it.

We found our old friends the Potteries doing duty here, and the lieutenant-colonel of the regiment was installed in the important post of resident, or representative of the Queen, under the superintendence of the Lord High Commissioner, a position conferring great power, even that of life and death. By him we were immediately installed in the government-home, and most hospitably entertained during the whole of our stay.

A further acquaintance with the town increased our surprise at its size and importance, in comparison with the extent of barren land and parched rock with which it was surrounded. A few arid attempts at gardens trenched upon the base of the

N

hill, and along shore a hedge or two of cactus and aloe refreshed the eye with spots of green. The barrack, military hospital, and a long, low, plain building, which does duty both as a church and schoolhouse, stand nearly in a line with each other, not far from the water's edge, at a short distance from the town, from which they are separated by a long piece of land levelled from the rock, and bearing a very parched unblessed appearance like a deserted stone-quarry. On one side, grilling on the shadeless level, stands the bronze statue of Sir Thomas Maitland, solitary and grim; while before him, equally hot, if not so dry and shiny, the troops in garrison defile on drill-days, or in the cool of the evening the beaux and belles of the city promenade to the music of the band. A tiny earthwork, mounting three guns, and paced by a solitary sentinel, alone breaks the monotonous line that overlooks the bay. This parade-ground is joined to the more antique portion of the town by a wide and smartly built street in the modern fashion; but many forlorn gaps attest that its completion must be a work of time.

I took an early opportunity of walking round the road called the little Jero, which, passing the parade-ground, circles the shoulder of the hill under which the city is built, and following the line of shore, but rising by a gradual ascent, turns abruptly off, and passing over the neck of the heights, surprises the stranger by the sudden view of the town lying at his feet at a distance of about half-a-mile. The great Jero is a prolongation of the same route; but instead of striking off and ascending the heights towards the interior, continues the forward road which reconducts it to the town by a circle of about fourteen miles in extent. On each side the way, the scanty red-brown soil is enclosed in patches by loose dwarf stone walls, and within them the currant-vine crawls along the surface like ground-ivy. Here and there a few olive-orchards, enclosed by high masonry, mark the spot where the earth lies a little deeper.

In the valleys and ravines, which remind one of the smaller spurs of the Cotswolds, white groups of cottages, edged with a little greenery, light up the view with a welcome prettiness, and near them may generally be remarked a few enclosures containing vines and tobacco. The picturesque and appropriate finish to such a landscape, in the shape of herds of goats of all sizes and colours, is never absent; there they dot the "herbless granite," or stand sentry on the splintered rocks, or crop the scanty mountain-weeds with a relish, till at eve they are driven into the town, which is entirely dependant on them for its supply of milk, their swollen udders teemful as of yore, when their grandams gave suck to the infant Jupiter,—classic

beasts, who alone in these lands have not degenerated since the days in which they were sung by
godlike poets, and sculptured by inspired hands.

Finding that my duties permitted me to take a
trip to Fort St George, I hired a carriage, and passing the whole length of the town of Argostoli, skirted
the shore of the creek, and passing the spot at
which it is spanned by a bridge, soon became
aware, through more senses than one, that the
water was rapidly degenerating into little better
than a swamp, wide, shallow, and encumbered with
weeds; and quite sufficient to account for the low
type of fever that is so fatal to the garrison and
inhabitants of Argostoli.   The valley I was
now pursuing was, however, evidently the richest
part of the island, and highly cultivated land
neatly enclosed on both sides, and good-looking
country houses with ornamental trees, and gardens
and olive-orchards, and here and there a few fruit-
trees, were quite a banquet to the eye wearied with
torrid barrenness.   After following the high road
for about two miles, I commenced a gradual
ascent of the hills, and a very different style of
country began to develop itself.   A group of
handsome pines especially attracted my attention
as a great novelty.   As I ascended higher, I
could fancy myself transported to some of the
heathery uplands of old England.   Undulating

hills clothed with a bright yellow flower, evidently
a species of furze, and here and there a few crumbling stone-walls, and a thorn-bush or two, through
which the clear mountain-breeze piped merrily,
and alive with the notes and movements of a little
bird resembling a titlark, made an appropriate
foreground for the frowning battlements of the
old castle I was nearing in front, and the grand
sombre mass and noble outline of the Black Mountain that loomed dark and cloud-capped on the left.

I soon arrived under the shadow of the fortress,
which crowned the summit of a very steep hill,
and, dismounting from the vehicle, clambered up
by a precipitous path that gained on the high road,
and found myself in the main street of the town
of St George, which consists of four parishes, and
could boast " long, long ago " of being the capital
of the island when the Venetians held sway, a time
when the strongest and wealthiest only felt secure
under the very guns of a friendly battery. Of this
town the four churches remain intact and in tolerable order, the black-robed Papa jangling his bells,
burning his pastiles, and chanting his ritual as
of yore; but alas! for the forsaken town. Weeds
choke the streets, fellest poverty rots amid the
ruins of palazzos once beautiful with sculpture and
wrought ironwork. Filthy rags flutter foully in
the air from rich carved balconies now crumbling to

their fall. A sickly and starved generation hold
forth the hand of beggary to the passing stranger
as he stumbles along the strange steep streets with
flights of steps in unexpected places, and so con-
fusedly and narrowly built that it is evident
that in its palmiest days the use of carriages in the
interior of the town must have been dispensed with.
In the hall of what had once been a house of importance, but cumbered now with reeking casks of
country wine, was a sinister-looking group of half-
starved peasants gambling by the aid of a filthy
pack of cards. I was glad to find myself at
the end of the broken pavement, and crossing the
antique drawbridge that gives entrance to the
castle. Here again was little beyond ruin; but
the ruins were grand, and the desolation bore a
proud and haughty aspect.

> " The roofless cot, decayed and rent,
>   Will scarce delay the passer by;
>   The tower by war or tempest bent,
>   While yet may frown one battlement,
>   Demands and daunts the stranger's eye.
>   Each ivied arch, and pillar lone,
>   Pleads haughtily for glories gone."

No one who has trod these deserted strongholds
of Venetian power, now crumbling in the grasp of
a more careless master, but must confess the vigour

and perseverance that are stamped in every vestige of their military occupation. It is not alone that tower and battlement, arch and buttress, defy by their intrinsic strength the assaults of time, and the vengeful hands of conquerors and levellers, but the relics of massive works in which the engineer's skill must have been tried to the utmost, and the builder must have built as builders have ceased to build now, are scattered profusely among their warlike trophies. In Corfu the attempt to level, by the means of gunpowder, a portion of their outworks, failed egregiously, and they stand yet a monument of their own tenacity, the grim old lion still stalking with expanded wings along the rent but still unruined bulwark. The fort of St George is a good specimen of their fortified works.

Its contracted area is cumbered with timeworn ruins of barracks, towers, and defensive structures, the battlements, arches, and covered ways remaining intact, save where the pickaxe of the destroyer has hewn its way, and numerous dwarf turrets cropping out from the turf, are but the vents of a magnificent system of tanks into which the ground beneath is quarried, and which must have served for the supply of a numerous garrison. A small portion of the buildings are kept in repair for the accommodation of a lieutenant's party of militia, and a gun or two, and a pretentious little pyramid of shot presided over by a sentry, are all the present munitions of defence of this once-renowned "tower upon the steep." The view all around is grand. On one side is a tolerably level plain of some fertility, with the white walls of a convent conspicuous in the distance, and having somewhat the appearance of an English farm. The sea usurps a large portion of the area of vision, its blue waters breaking in foam against the sterile rocks that swell rearward till they culminate in the Black Mountain, the Athos of the ancients, a resting-place for the clouds. The road by which I came is traceable like a wavy white riband to the very port of Argostoli, and the sails of the vessels are visible within its land-locked basin.

After partaking of the hospitality of the worthy commandant, who has reversed the motto of " cedant arma togæ," I set out to return. As I was sauntering down the road, a young girl left the door of a cottage that clung like a martin's nest to the rock above, and descending with a slow listless step held out for my acceptance a small bunch of wild flowers. The face was perfect Grecian in its contour, and her garments, though denoting great poverty, could not conceal an exquisite figure. I rewarded her gift by the present of a shilling, unromantic in itself, I confess, but accompanied by the most Sir Charles Grandison air I could muster.

She was, however, by no means killed by it, but pocketed the coin off-hand, without moving a muscle of expression, and turning on her heel reascended the hill without once casting a glance below, and disappeared within the cottage. I have often noticed this strange kind of apathy among the Greek poor. The possession of a shilling is rare among the class she represented, and I am convinced that had the gift been munificent her demeanour would have been the same. I was in hopes of coaxing a smile from so pretty a mouth, and could not help being much amused at my own disappointment.

I had not time to attempt the ascent of the Black Mountain, which I am informed would well repay the time and trouble. Those who have scaled its heights tell of beautiful groves of pine, and grand scenery like that of the Highlands of Scotland, and ravines in which the snow lies deep in wreathed drifts. The Cephalonians pride themselves greatly on these pines, which appear to grow with peculiar regularity, and though they never much exceed thirty feet in height, are very shapely. Specimens of the young trees carefully peeled and polished, are all the fashion for hat-stands in the neighbouring islands, and are very ornamental. They are also much used as walking-sticks, the wood being at the same time compact and light.

I found time to take a walk across the singular

obstruction which I mentioned as forming so conspicuous an object from the bay. I found it to be
a long pile of masonry, half causeway and half
bridge, with a small obelisk near the centre. The
current toiled languidly through the arches, and logs
of wood, weeds, and other obtrusive rubbish, ebbed
and flowed with the sluggish water. This bridge
is famous in island-history for a successful defence
made by a sergeant and twelve men of Her Majesty's
Thirty-sixth Regiment against a numerous and well-
armed body of rebels, who had suddenly descended
from the hills, for the purpose of seizing the town,
in eighteen hundred and forty-eight. The assail-
ants [suffered severely, and five English soldiers
were killed and wounded.

On quitting the bridge, I came upon the foot
of the barren range of hills that had so startled
me with their baked and dreary appearance on
my first arrival, but immediately fronting me
was a little oasis nestling in a tiny ravine
that pierced the rock. An avenue of spreading plane-trees led to a more than usually pretty
and cleanly kept Greek chapel, and a few paces
further brought me to the white walls of the English burying-ground. Passing through a guard-
house,—for, alas! the graves of heretics cannot be
left here without military protection,—I entered a
square plot of ground about two acres in extent.
There were several monuments that arrested the

eye by their size and decorated character, especially a slender graceful column of considerable height, which bore the traces of wanton injury. A few small ornamental shrubs were scattered about; but the most pleasing feature was the beauty and profusion of the geranium-beds that covered the last resting-places of the dead. A vigorous growth of aloes usurped a large space of the ground, their huge coarse leaves battling with each other for room, and domineering over every speck of adjacent soil. These monsters, that seemed the very emblems of robust vitality, were once tiny plants, set to mark the grave of some departed comrade, but as the poor relic of mortality wasted beneath, the sapling above shot into vigorous life, rejoicing in its native soil and climate, spreading over the neighbouring graves, and drawing sustenance from the corruption below.

As I stood contemplating this peculiar spot, on casting my eyes upward they were arrested by the bare bleak head of a lofty hill, piercing wedge-like into the sky, and seeming to almost overhang the place on which I stood. As the sun poured its resistless rays on it, it glowed like a dome of metal, flecked with calcined streaks as though the colours had run from intense heat, and it must have flashed them on the molten sea below, and the baked and blistering roofs of the town that basked beneath its influence; but here all was cool and green, and the eye rejoiced in its circumscribed territory of flower and shrub.

There is one curiosity in this island which, as it lies but a short distance from the town, few strangers depart without inspecting. A stream, which is now arrested by a mill-dam and forced into the service of man, being compelled to turn an undershot wheel for him and grind corn, runs in a broad and rapid channel from the sea, losing itself in three Plutonic-looking caverns, into which it rushes gurgling, to find vent—where? Ay, there's the rub. Philosophers have speculated in vain, and waifs of all kinds, from a dead bullock to a gallon of oil, have been thrown in, in hopes of a reappearance somewhere; but not so much as a horn or a hoof or a globule has ever made sign again. As I gazed into the jagged mouths of this abyss, I conjured up strange visions of whirlpools à la Schiller—the bowels of the earth, as lectured on by savants and displayed to our gaze in pantomimes—central fire, as particularized in the last sermon of the Reverend Jedediah Howler—a delicious hole for a murderer in a large line of business, *vide* Ainsworth, Reynolds, and Co., and other gnome-like horrors, and I confessed that there was more between earth's surface and its centre than was ever dreamed of in my philosophy.

Our time now drew to a close, and the first rays

of the morning sun gilded the spires of Argostoli just as we steamed out of the creek, between the shelving limestone of the mountains within whose hot embrace, cabined, cribbed, confined, the unlucky inhabitants were soon to swelter. Not all that kindness and unbounded hospitality could do for us could prevent a sensation of relief in quitting its shores, or in acknowledging the justice of the Italian motto, "Cephalonia, melanchonia." We soon crossed the bay, passing within sight of the livelier and rival town of Luxuri; but it was long past noon ere the limb-like spurs of the naked rocks of Cephalonia had been left behind, deforming the waters like the fossil skeleton of some monstrous kraken of the world before the flood.

CHAPTER XIX.

FEW were the officers of the Corfu garrison who did not pay a visit, impelled by a love of sport or from simple curiosity, to the ruins of Butrinto, the Buthrotum of the ancients, where, as the guide-book learnedly informs us, " Æneas was entertained by his kinsman Hercules." Through the kindness of the Lord High Commissioner I was enabled to see it, rose-tinted, having received an invitation to attend him and Lady Young on an expedition to that port, for the purpose of selecting horses for purchase from the Albanians, who by previous arrangement had assembled there to meet him. A three hours' sail in a yacht, with the Acroceraunian mountains in all their iron-bound grandeur on our right, and the more majestic and graceful St Salvador on our left, brought us to the entrance of a river that wound in mazes between low reedy banks, desolate in aspect and covered with scrub-wood. Disembarking from our yachts at the bar of the river, we transferred ourselves to a little flotilla, manned by the crews of the official magnates of Corfu. A three-mile pull brought us to the old castle of Butrinto, its solid Venetian walls scarred by time, and looking the very picture of neglect, and disfigured by a shabby attempt at rendering one of its massive towers habitable, in the worst possible style, and with the most incongruous materials. Here was stationed a Turkish aga, with a guard of about a hundred Albanian soldiers, a large portion of whom were militia. The regulars, save the mark, were drawn up in a sort of line to receive us, and opened on us a straggling fire, which was intended as a salute.

The first object that attracted our attention on landing was a mass of mangy-looking wool spread to dry, and three or four poverty-stricken women, the wrinkled parchment of their faces only partially concealed by dirty white veils, were pulling and stretching it to expose it more thoroughly to the action of the sun. The guardians now opened on us, and commended total abstinence from all contact with the said wool or women, under penalty of incarceration in Quarantine Island on our return. Somehow I saw a good deal of this same pestiferous wool sticking to the shoes of more than one of the party, but providentially neither the delinquents themselves nor the island of Corfu were stricken with either plague or cholera in consequence. A walk of a few furlongs brought us to the place of meeting, a vast plain covered with half-burnt brush-wood and coarse grass, and tenanted by a herd of large cream-coloured oxen, the property of the contractor of the Corfu garrison. Our observation soon became concentrated on the wild troops of horses and wilder men who now surrounded us. Dirty and tattered, but the costume Albanian and graceful in its very rags and ruin; with the forepart of the head shaved, and unkempt elfin raven locks escaping from the fez - entangled masses behind, their sparkling eyes and gipsy faces wild with excitement, as they tugged at the bridles of their little wiry and hard-bitted horses; these children of the Highland passes formed the foreground of a picture unique in its meet accessories of river, mountain, and ruined fortress.

All concerned in horse-flesh were soon in high deal; the guardians having once opened their mouths, and reminded us that leather, rope, and clothing were all plague and cholera—a pleasant intimation to men who were grappling at the mouths of restless ponies, and being hustled by their masters—and thereby delivered themselves of their duty, had sense enough to shut their eyes, and drop the curtain on the farce for the rest of the day. Two or three lithe light-weight Albanians acted as jockeys, and scrambling on pony-back with their knees nearly on a level with the withers, their feet hidden in enormous stirrups, the bottoms of which ended in a point to act as a spur, darted off in true beggar-on-horseback style, shouting and cracking their whips, and after a whirligig gallop the poor beast returned panting and terrified, and was pulled up short on his haunches in front of us. The ponies were all of one breed, wiry fiery little Arabs, their general colour grey, less than half broken, and few but bore the marks of rough usage. If any one of them in particular proved troublesome or seemed to betray the secrets of his temper, his master, fearful of his indiscretion, would quietly advance his mouth to the erring beast's ear, and apparently whisper into it something cabalistic, short, and marvellously to the purpose, that reduced him at once to a demeanour of decent hypocrisy. We were puzzled to account for so magical a process, but at length observed that a little blood was left on the lips, and that the whole secret lay in a good bite. Verily a new way of taming a shrew.

While this scene was enacting, the picturesque barbarians crowded around us. Scarce a man was unarmed, but here and there an individual arrested our attention by some distinctive peculiarity. A quiet whey-faced fellow, with a good-humoured but weak smile, and without a hair

o

of beard or whisker on his fat cheek, with a white turban on his head, and clothed from neck to heel in a robe of light blue coarse cloth, like a dressing-gown, was prominent among the group of our admirers. Fastened to his girdle was a silver inkstand and a sheath for pens. This personage, I was informed, was the aga's secretary with his tools of office. A very handsome little boy, the orphan son of a man of distinction and heir of a large property, who was destined, as we were told, to receive his education in England, was here as a spectator under the guidance of a tutor,—such a tutor! who treated his charge with the greatest respect, and never left his side for a moment, holding assiduously over his head a large green cotton umbrella of a very Gamp-like character. He was not over cleanly in person, and dressed in a mongrel Albanian costume, with a close-fitting skull-cap on his head, which did not show to advantage a set of plain features, and a nose which some bygone bout of fight or frolic had reduced to the shape of the letter S, from each side of which a pair of piggish eyes kept each other in view across the broken bridge.

When I had sufficiently enjoyed the bustle and humour of this novel horse-fair, I joined a party that were about to start for a row on the lake of Butrinto. Crossing the river, the boat was thrust through a narrow channel almost choked with mud,

a forest of gigantic reeds closing us in on both
sides, and nearly meeting above our heads. We
had just begun to feel somewhat tired of this
amphibious progression, when the boat suddenly
emerged on a vast silent lake, edged green with
beds of rushes, and set in a rugged frame of bare
majestic mountains. Not a bark or thing of life
floated on its huge expanse of silver sheen or
mountain shadow, but by fits the startled mallard
would whir upward from his screen of reeds, and
a white shining apparition, in the shape of a long
lustrous kind of fish, was constantly leaping several
feet out of water, and turning a somersault, would
come down broadside on, with a flap that made
the bright drops rise in a shower, and descend in
specks of foam,—a delightful way, doubtless, of
spending a summer's afternoon in these latitudes.

All looked so weird and desolate, that the imagination did not hesitate to acknowledge the plausi-
bility, at least, of the legend of the enchanted fish
in the hundred-and-one nights, and I began to wish
myself fairly out of such suspicious waters, and had
we come across a floating bottle, I am sure I should
never have dared open it, for fear of an unpleasant
mist, and an evil genius, and a notice to quit and
go overboard, all in scales, and sporting a tail, and
nothing left in life but to cut somersaults in fine
weather. After an hour's sail, we rethreaded our

way to the river, and as soon as I began to breathe
freely, my reflections took a turn dinner-ward, a
sensation all the more delightful, when the Sentient
feels assured that a good repast is somewhere or
other in store for him. We soon collected our
party, and keeping the same side of the river, and
crossing a little scrap of bog, just sufficiently serious
to enable adventurous knights-errant to do a trifle
in the Raleigh line in behalf of their dames, we
ascended an abrupt declivity to a space of broken
ground, all knolls and shrubs, and green with
myrtle, and pied with asphodel, and alive with
humming bees ; and scattered profusely amid the
whole, usurped by a host of fragrant creepers, or
half-hidden by ranker shrubs, or sternly facing us,
tall, rent, and bare, lay the ruins of an ancient
city. Not a mere mouldering quarry of shattered
stone, nor scraps of crumbling nothingness, to be
pondered over by the antiquary, but solid enduring
arches, towers unroofed and rifted, but still square
to the storm, and battling bravely with time and
decay, and lording it still over their connecting
lines of circumvallation, as when they held watch
and ward over them of yore, with their guard of
slingers and archers, and the mailed warriors of a
Roman legion.

Such is all that now remains of the city of
Butrinto. Climbing the rugged edges of one of

the towers, I gazed over a wide extent of desolate beauty. Below me slept the calm sullen expanse of the lake, watched over by the mountains, its rugged warders. The sinuous river laved the time-worn castle, while around it lounged the armed groups of uncouth warriors, half-soldiers, half-banditti, garbed as in the day when the towers of their fortress, with its foreign garrison, first rose to lord it over the conquered territory.

Under a wide-spreading fig-tree, we now sacrificed freely to the shade of Apicius, and astonished the old gods of Greece by libations of iced champagne, the which, if they snuffed up as freely as it was poured, there must have been a grand night of it hard by on Olympus. At length some unimpassioned prudent soul, such as the god who presides over pic-nics seems always to have at hand for the salvation of his votaries, warned us that the sunlight was waning, and reforming the procession, we were soon in our boats, and awaiting the signal to dip the oars. The Albanian guard had by this time assembled to do us honour, and again an irregular discharge of fire-arms woke the solitary echoes. Close by me a stalwart artillery-man was holding on to the decaying posts of the landing-place by his boat-hook, and I was much amused by hearing him mutter with a vicious earnestness, "I should like to tackle half-a-dozen of them there chaps with this here boat-hook." At length we were fairly off, and a few strokes carried us into the quiet solitude of the reedy desert that stretched on both sides.

As I gave a parting look rearward, a scene displayed itself that will never be erased from my mind's eye. The sun had sunk, and a broad rosy circle usurped the western horizon, and in the midst of it stood forth the gloomy walls of the old fortress, the terrible blood-red flag of the Turk floating on its summit. As I watched this picture of solemn beauty, a tall figure, draped in flowing robes of white, stole forth from the cover of the tower, and seated itself on the verge of the battlement. This was the mufti, the Turkish priest. Beside him, within reach of his hand, a small white object stood motionless, and I could scarcely believe my senses when I recognised it to be a stork, asleep with his head under his wing, and resting on one leg. Presently, however, a second, a third, and a fourth, came slowly winging their way home, and these strange silent sentries took up their position in line, and made themselves comfortable for the night. Ruin, and silence, and sleep, and the deepening shades of night—and amid this ominous conjunction, the crimson folds of the Turkish ensign descended slowly from the staff.

The Turks regard the stork with a superstitious

reverence, and are accustomed to connect the tenure of their power over a territory with the presence of these birds; and it is affirmed that they have followed the footsteps of the Moslem, in retreat or advance, with strange pertinacity. The Sultan's enemies suggest, that as the favourite food of the stork consists of snakes, the loss of his tid-bits drives him by dint of cultivation before the approach of advancing humanity. In Greece, where they once abounded, scarce a solitary straggler is to be seen, and yet no one can deny that in Greece there is wilderness enough for the gratification of reptiles. The truth is, the stork is a silent old-fashioned feathered biped, with much affinity to his kind solemn old friend of the crescent, at whose side he is welcome to doze in safety, while a couple of chattering restless Greeks would fidget the most passionless of storks into fits and an early grave.

We had now been quartered above a year in Corfu, and the old circle of duties and amusements began to commence anew. Once more the swamps of Potarno were studded with tents, and the butts riddled with musket-balls. Again St Spiridion, commonly called St Spiro, equivalent in our tongue to calling St John St Jack, made his accustomed circuit by day and night. The scene on the esplanade was, however, somewhat changed. Peace had now become an accomplished fact, and in place of two regiments of the line drilling their best, in the hope of soon confronting a formidable enemy, peaceful contests with bat and ball were daily waged; and seldom has livelier or more spirited play been seen, than was daily exhibited between the elevens selected from the different regiments. Tents were pitched, and on many occasions bands added the attraction of music, and ladies honoured us with their presence, while the gallant proprietor of Carter's hotel would exercise his four-in-hand team of greys through the avenues.

Those were merry days, and the climate was like an English summer, and the turf was soft and green, and the sun spared us for a season, ere he gathered strength for future revenge. The most amusing match was one played between an eleven selected from the garrison, and sixteen Tritons and Modestes. Not that the said Triton swore green hair and scaly tails, and blew a shell apiece, or that the Modestes were so encumbered with bashfulness as to appear in veils and refuse to answer questions. No; the said sixteen were jolly and worthy specimens of the genus Jack Tar who had just pulled ashore from two men-of-war lying in harbour. The game commenced by the sailors taking their innings, and they made a good fight of it, and hit away the straightest balls from the very bails, and rushed and shouted like true Britons as they were, and not being troubled with nervousness ran up a good score, and their scorer, a young middy, did his best to help them by adding on twenty without being discovered. They possessed several advantages, and made the most of them. The swiftest ball glanced from their shins as from an iron bar, and though they all played with naked feet, the most ripping bowler might drop it on them with as little effect as if they had been roots of heart of oak. The eleven against whom they had to contend were very formidable, and Jack had to strike his flag, but not as long as a stick, in the shape of a wicket, would stand. Hatless and shoeless, they fielded with an energy that deserved better luck, and in the intervals allowed for rest solaced themselves with a game of leap-frog.

CHAPTER XX.

ON Tuesday the fifteenth of April, Her Majesty's ship Caradoc steamed into harbour, bringing orders for the Royal Blanks to hold themselves in readiness to embark for Zante, and relieve their old allies, the Red Roses, ordered home. All was now on the *qui vive*, and a few hours would have sufficed to have marched the men on board, but it was not till the afternoon of the seventh of May that the flag, that telegraphed the approach of a transport steamer, was run up to the mast-head of the signal station; and hurrying from a luxurious couch on the grass, watching a cricket-match, I hastened to the shore and saw the huge hull of the Peninsular and Oriental Company's steamer Columbo looming in the distance, and before sunset she came to anchor in the port.

The preparations for the movement of a regiment produce a scene of excitement and confusion general and individual. The commandant issues orders which shake the economy of the regiment to its very centre like little earthquakes, and appal the stoutest hearts. The senior officer has not a word for his dearest friend except about shop, and is constantly in quest of the adjutant. The adjutant takes fire, and inflames the orderly-room, whose clerks and orderlies scribble and rush right and left. The quarter-master is constantly sent for, but rarely found, oscillating about the barracks, and into every possible and impossible hole and corner, stained with the variation of each soil, black, white, and grey of every conceivable store and cupboard, with a note-book in his hand, a pencil between his teeth, and docketed files of official papers protruding from all his pockets, and followed by a barrack-sergeant, an ordnance-clerk, a tradesman with a bill, a soldier's wife the worse for liquor, and the contract-butcher, with each of whom he has a separate quarrel, which they respectively insist shall be settled on the instant, and to their own satisfaction.

Lord Byron bemoans the " sweat, dust, and blasphemy of packing." Fancy the packing of seven hundred men, with stores public and private, bag, baggage, and baggages. The soldiers' pets themselves are no joke to travel with. No profession accumulates a greater portion of live lumber

in that shape than that of the soldier. Dogs get
nervous and excited on the eve of a march. Their
tails can settle down to nothing for an instant, and
they never stir from the regimental heels, fearful of
being left behind. Cats, on the contrary, levant
incontinently, clinging to their Lares and Penates,
and feeling a something sacred in the tiles on which
they have so long "lived and loved together," and
are conveyed on board fast bound in baskets and
pillow-cases.

On Monday the twenty-first, a company embarked on board Her Majesty's ship Triton to
garrison the island of Santa Maura; and a detachment under the command of a subaltern proceeded
by the same conveyance to Cerigo, the Leucadia
and Cytherea of the olden time.

On the tenth of May, at two P.M., the Royal
Blanks mustered for the last time on their old
parade-ground. Two men only of the whole regiment had unfitted themselves for duty, and the
men being told off, and the band of the Metropoli-
tans fallen in in addition to their own, they marched
left in front through the esplanade, the scene of
their fourteen months' service, and were soon drawn
up in two lines along the edge of the castle-ditch
where they had disembarked on their arrival. Now
came adieus, and cheers returning cheers. Old
grudges were forgotten, old quarrels forgiven, and,

as barge after barge pushed slowly from the shore, the cheers of the men were answered by their comrades on the ramparts and our old friends the jolly tars of the Modeste. A short time sufficed to make all snug aboard the fine roomy steamer which was now our home for a few days at least, and at daybreak next morning we got under weigh.

None of us could gaze upon the lovely shores of Corfu, as for the last time we coasted along their woodland heights, without a feeling of regret, arising from the reminiscences of fourteen months spent among scenes of beauty and gaiety, and with as few memorials of sorrow as could well fall to the lot of human beings. The bluff headland, on which shone the snow-white walls of the convent of Peliogestriza, was the last point to bid us farewell, and pleasant were the memories it recalled. The islands of Paxo and Antipaxo were soon passed, and on our lee shore the white cliffs of Santa Maura and the rock whence Sappho took her fatal leap hang yet over the abyss. Then the mountainous line of the Grecian continent once more opened on us, and " Suli's rock and Parga's shore " were duly pointed out and admired. Then again came the barbarous stony waste of Cephalonia, with Ithaca hiding coyly in its rear. The entrance to the bay, whence runs the creek on which Argostoli is built, was marked by its lighthouse, and I had the satisfaction of recognising my old friend Fort George, like an eagle's nest on the brow of the mountain. Ere the sun set we had a good view of the wavy outline of a lofty well-wooded island which was soon to be our home, and its rich appearance contrasted well with the sterile shores along which we had been so long coasting.

The sun had sunk, and the short twilight of these climes had deepened into night, ere we cast anchor in the bay of Zante. An amphitheatre of twinkling lights lay level with the water's edge, and high in air the lamp of a signal-station glittered like a planet. Boats had already come alongside, and a detachment of officers were soon on board, anxious to get forward the preparations for to-morrow's work. In anticipation of a busy day we retired early, and morning had scarcely dawned ere we were on deck surveying our new place of abode. The town of Zante is so situated as to enable the eye to take in the whole of its main features at a glance. The houses lie in the shape of an irregular crescent, accommodating themselves to the curve of the bay; and in rear of them a steep and lofty hill rises to a great height, its summit adorned with a mural crown of fortifications, presided over by the Union Jack; and a signal-station, with its usual spider-web apparatus of poles and ropes, with black balls and little fluttering flags for flies, occupying one of the bastions.

On the left, as you face the town from the sea, rises a lofty green hill, its verdant sides sown with cottages, and the white walls of a convent glittering in a hollow, just below the highest point, on which, upright like a horn, in clear relief against the sky, is a singularly shaped knuckle of rock that imparts a somewhat comic expression to its otherwise graceful proportions. This hill is called Scopo, and in its bosom are contained the treasures of water that bestow an artificial freshness on the arid streets of Zante. On the right of the town is a bold headland crowned with a waving garment of luxuriant olive-trees, the ravine that divides it from the castle-hill green and bright with orange and other garden trees, and dotted with white chapels and cottages. A stone jetty, irregular in shape, projects from about the centre of the town into the sea, and moored under its protection lies a little fleet of merchantmen of all nations and most diverse rig. In rear of this jetty an avenue of dwarf trees marks the situation of the esplanade and drill-ground, beside which is a clump of buildings of some pretension, on one of which the eternal and infernal yellow flag is flaunting spitefully, marking it as the head-quarters of the island authorities. In its general aspect the town has

much in common with that of Argostoli, but several
of the chapel spires are of a superior order of
architecture, and possess an additional charm in
retaining the natural colour of their stone, which is
a rich brown. The space between the shore and
the castle-hill is evidently very contracted, for
we could observe that the houses in the rear partook
of its elevation, and had begun to climb its sides.

It having been determined that the men should
not disembark till the next day, we seized the opportunity of stealing ashore, and, hiring a carriage,
commenced a voyage of discovery. We found the
majority of the streets to be narrow and crooked,
and paved with broad slabs of stone which dipped
towards the centre, forming at once a road and a
drain. We soon, however, escaped from the town,
and, rattling over a good macadamised way, began
to ascend the hill that leads to the castle, skirting
the ravine that separates it from the woodland
heights that form the district called Acroteria.
We were much pleased with all we saw. Cleanliness and industry, and an appearance of an advanced
condition of agriculture, met us on every side. No
cottage in Devonshire could be whiter or cleaner
than many we saw, and gardens, the pictures of
care and neatness, were enclosed within white-
washed walls, save where every stone was hid by
hedges of pomegranate and oleander, interspersed

with the pale green arrows of the feathery bamboo.
Orange and fig trees, cherry-orchards and mulberry-
bushes grew in profuse but well-ordered variety,
and beneath the groves of the olive-tree, which is
here carefully tended, pruned, and manured, golden
crops of barley were just ready for the sickle, and
children, armed with a primitive clapper composed
of a split bamboo, were scaring away the birds.
Patches of aloe and cactus caught the eye at intervals, and the frequent vision of the wavy plumes
of a palm gave an oriental character to the prospect.
Future experience confirmed our first impression
of the industrious character of the natives. The
women weave and knit with unflagging perseverance, and tiny children collect manure from the
roads in little baskets. In short, a transition from
Corfu to Zante resembles turning over a page of
Hogarth from the idle to the industrious appren-
tice.

After a winding ascent of about half-a-mile we
reached the head of the ravine, and found a road
crossing ours at right angles. Pursuing the branch
that led to the right we continued the ascent for a
few hundred yards, and were then on the heights
of Acroteri. Leaving on the left a handsome house,
whose tall proportions were almost concealed by a
wilderness of oleanders that dazzled the eye, we
passed along a road, bounded on one side by a vine-

P

yard, and on the other by groves of olive, and in
a few minutes drew up opposite the chateau of
Acroteri.

I will here take the opportunity to explain that
the town of Zante contained no quarters for officers,
who were thereby compelled to rent houses in the
town or its vicinity; and as this chateau fell afterwards into my hands, and as it affords a good
specimen of the ancient country-houses in Zante, I
will anticipate the course of my narrative to give a
description of it.

The centre compartment was three stories in
height, and surmounted by a gable roof, the front
of which was concealed by a curvilinear battlement
of stone, on the summit and both ends of which
three rusty iron vanes were fixed as ornaments on
stone balls. A large and handsome portico on
arches, built of polished limestone, and surmounted
by a handsome balustrade, projected twelve feet in
front above the principal entrance, and rose to a
level with the first floor, the windows of which
opened upon it; and when covered with an awning, it formed a delightful out-of-doors apartment.
On entering the house, you found yourself in a
lofty airy hall, above it another room of the same
dimensions, and above that were four sleeping-
apartments besides attics for lumber. On the sides
of this centre were two wings reaching to the height

of the first story, that on the left containing two large rooms one above the other, and that on the right divided into smaller compartments, consisting of the kitchen and other offices. Doors and windows were large and numerous, and below the ground-floor were spacious cellars, so contrived that they could be used as stables. The chateau was well constructed of limestone, and had been erected by a Venetian nobleman; and throughout the principal points of bearing, strong clamps of iron gripped the stonework to resist the strain of the shocks of earthquake that are so prevalent in these islands.

An old Venetian chateau would lose half its interest if not identified with its tale of horror, and very few of the Greeks, high or low, would be tempted to pass the night alone in a certain room in Chateau Acroteri. That dark deeds were once committed there all protest, and that a man-fiend with a huge head, speechless, but with scowls and gestures too demoniac to bear description, rises and threatens the luckless intruder, is as well authenticated as any other ghost-story. I once examined the apartment narrowly in hopes to discover some solution to the mystery. It was a small oblong whitewashed room, well lit by two windows. It had been long disused, and retained that hot mouldy atmosphere so well adapted to induce nightmare.

On one side, high on the wall, was a small window secured by a wooden shutter, which I found communicated with the roof of one of the wings, and through this aperture it would doubtless be easy for a mischievous person to terrify a nervous occupant. In many respects the house was well adapted to mystify the believer in the marvellous to his heart's content. The numerous doors and windows were much out of repair, and the wood-work had shrunk, splitting into crannies for the sighing of the wind. Every window had its accompanying set of jalousies as well as a pair of shutters, and to every shutter and jalousie were attached catches of iron, both to hold them back against the walls when open, and clamp them together when shut. The whole of these fastenings, including the bolts and latches of the doors, were of ponderous iron-work of the most primitive pattern, and by lapse of time, and rust and wear, had become loose and rickety. Fancy a Levanter rioting among this rattle-trap collection. The howlings and chains of a hundred ghosts could not be worse. There was also something peculiar in the building that caused the wind to imitate now and then the creaking sound of footsteps; and, on one occasion, as I sat reading, I distinctly heard some one advance along the passage, and after halting at the door, retire again. I took no notice of this for the first and second time, but as it occurred once more, I felt annoyed by the intrusion, and followed the retreating footsteps just in time to be convinced that the said somebody was just nobody. Had this happened at midnight instead of at noon, I confess I should have tumbled into bed with the least possible delay.

Forlorn and ghostified as the interior of the mansion was, light and beauty was spread around its exterior. On three sides it was surrounded by gardens, walled in, and covered with the foliage of the fig, orange, vine, lemon, cherry, and mulberry, among which were bushes of myrtle, oleander, and pomegranate; and clinging to a dilapidated trellis-work at the rear of the house, was a complete mass of passion-flower, green and vigorous as ivy, and spangled with a constant succession of blossom. The garden in front had originally been of considerable size and beauty. A line of vases containing flowers was ranged along the top of the entrance-wall, and on the successive levels of six terraces, to which access was gained by descending flights of nine steps each, flowers and shrubs still struggled to exist among the bushes and fruit-trees that had begun to supplant them. The relics of a pretty fountain lay half-hidden beneath weeds and rubbish, the limpid spring still stealing forth, while pedestals on which statues once stood were now occupied by hollow trunks of trees which here serve the purpose of bee-hives.

But the real beauty of Acroteri consisted in its situation; and if you will step out with me to the front of the portico, I will attempt a description of it. High on the left hand, towering above an olive-grove, at a distance of about a mile and a half, though an air-line would diminish the distance by at least a third, standing forth in strong relief against the sky, is the summit of the castle-hill, its store of barracks, chapels, magazines, and hospital rising one above another in rear of a line of lofty ramparts. A far horizon, shaped from mazy ridges of hills of a hazy blue, and lower apparently than the castle, carries the eye forward to the centre of the landscape, their bases lost to view in valleys hidden by an intervening curtain of high fore-ground richly clothed with olive-trees, and which, sloping in varied undulations, extends downwards in a wavy line of verdure to meet the seashore on the right centre of the picture I am attempting to delineate. This wide-spread carpet of waving woodland would of itself be an element of beauty, but in this instance it is chequered and heightened in effect by the white walls of villas, cottages, and farm-buildings gleaming through it, together with numerous gardens, in which the glorious dark polished foliage of the orange, sown with golden stars, contrasts well with the shifting grey green of the olive. The spire-shaped cypress, here in groups and there in lines of avenues, shoots to a height the loftiest firs in England seldom exceed, the grey varnished trunks of the patriarchs shining forth from their veil of sombre leaves. On the right, the Mediterranean, basking in the sun-glare, or leaping in purple waves crested with foam under the influence of the fitful breezes of the Levant, bears on its bosom the white sails of fishing-craft or tall merchantman, or is ploughed into paths of molten silver by the paddle-wheels of the passing steamer.

Beautiful as is the aspect of these bright waters, they have little semblance to a sea, but rather bear the borrowed likeness of a noble lake girt with glowing shores, and broken by isle and promontory, so land-locked is it to all appearance by the coast of Greece and intervening islands. A grand and noble object, swelling in bold outline from the azure wave that laves its base, rises the dark mass of the Black Mountain of Cephalonia, at a distance of about eight miles, the gloomy hue of its robe of pines standing forth distinctly in contrast with the torrid glare of the limestone flecked in spots with the greenish brown of its spare patches of cultivation. Looming over its shoulder, hazy in the distance, is the lofty peak of Ithaca, and groups of nameless island-rocks, jagged in shape, stand like grim sentries before the

low but stony cliffs that mark the shore of the
Morea. Still further to the right, and far inland,
rise the blue indistinct peaks of Parnassus ; and
on the brow of a hill near the shore, the ruined but
still imposing feudal tower of Castle Tornese frowns
over the desolate territory it once held in sway.

Close to the entrance of Acroteri was a long
whitewashed cottage of one story, and roofed, as all
buildings are here, with fluted tiles. Half its length
was devoted to a room in which miscellaneous agricultural implements, stores, and poultry were wont
to congregate. One room sufficed for the family,
consisting of an old couple, a young man with his
wife and baby, and three boys from seventeen to
seven. These good folks had been left in charge
of the house and gardens, the latter of which they
rented, and in addition kept among the neighbouring olive-groves a large flock of sheep and goats.
A lean old horse and a pet donkey, three half-
starved watch-dogs and two ditto cats, with a
numerous tribe of poultry, completed the establishment.

In ordinary times the whole family snored the
night through gregariously on shelves and benches;
a sickly goat or two, or sheep with a cold in its
head, being occasionally made at home for the night
in the family circle; but when the June sun was
beginning to drive his heat-beams into the earth,

I one morning observed the males of the family chattering and gesticulating in the corner of the garden over a heap of boughs, bamboo-rods, and a stout pole or two; and by degrees this bundle of rubbish was manipulated into a sort of arbour, or box of greens, raised about four feet from the ground, with a kind of pigeon-hole entrance big enough to admit a man crawling in by help of a short ladder. Here the lords of this creation used to enjoy their siesta, and pass the close hot nights of summer, combining the *utile* of guarding their fruit with the *dulce* of a cool snooze.

In justice to the Greek peasantry, I must here state that the interiors of the larger number of cottages are kept scrupulously clean; and the bed, which is usually a four poster, is an especial object of pride. If the owner has been rich enough to retain any remnants of his heir-looms in the shape of Greek lace, it will be seen displayed around the hangings, or on the edges of the counterpane. A small ornament in the form of a cross invariably occupies the space at the head, and knots of riband, and shapes cut in coloured cloth, are sewn upon the curtains and valance. The interior of the bed-clothes unluckily does not always bear such close inspection.

CHAPTER XXI.

I MUST now return on board, where I left the regiment taking their ease in their own ship, and next day, the thirteenth, at twelve o'clock, after having their dinners on board, the men once more buckled on their knapsacks and prepared to disembark. A little fleet of barges, of smaller size than those of Corfu, soon conveyed us to the mole, and three companies immediately proceeded to march up to the castle, and take possession of the barracks there, the rest with the staff and colours remaining in the town. The wing whose destination was the castle, commenced ascending the hill, and soon met the division of the Red Roses, whose quarters they were about to occupy. On reaching the cross roads, they turned to the left, leaving Acroteri to the rear.

The road gradually becomes steeper and steeper, but leads through a very pretty country, with large ornamental gardens and neat cottages on each side, that cluster into a village as we approach the gate of the castle. The road begins at length to wind about in true engineering style, now giving us a view of the vales and woodlands of the interior, and now taking us to the edge of the steep cliffs that overhang the town of Zante, the houses, bay, and shipping lying like toys at our feet. The march got now to be excessively wearisome, and we were glad enough when we found ourselves passing under the first archway; but a steep twist or two of hill still remained ere we had gone through the second and were fairly within the precincts of the castle. We then discovered that the interior of the fortress was nearly as steep as its outward approach, and it required a sturdy pull ere we found ourselves drawn up in line in front of the range of barrack-rooms that formed one side of the contracted space that had been levelled into a parade-ground.

The men divested themselves at once of their knapsacks and piled their arms, but several hours elapsed before we were able to get them shaken into their barrack-rooms. The giving over of barrack-rooms from one regiment to another, under the superintendence of the quarter-master and his assistants, is always a most tedious and trying operation. The quarter-master of the outgoing regiment is ever at his wits' end to prove that every article left in the rooms is in the most clean, orderly, and sound condition, and the barrack-sergeant acts as leading counsel on the other side ; while the quarter-master of the incoming regiment refuses to take anything over, until it has been decided whether its defects are to be made 'good by the regiment that is quitting or by the barrack-department. On entering one of the rooms I found the authorities in full debate, as to whether certain scraps of wood and a hoop or two of rusty iron did or did not constitute a perfect bucket. The energy with which the counsel for the Red Roses protested that these elements properly combined would turn out a bucket complete, seemed quite to overwhelm a quiet old sergeant, who held his brief on the other side, and he could do little more than finger the said elements with a puzzled and hopeless look. I had no business to interfere, and as I had seen more than once a common sheet of foolscap turned into a lantern, a currycomb, a bishop's wig, a cradle, a cathedral window, and a host of other articles of use and ornament, I might have had some hesitation in deciding the point. At length, just before sundown we succeeded in getting the three companies housed for the night.

It was some time before we got well acquainted with our new abode. The battlements enclosed an area of about fourteen acres, standing on a steep acclivity, and presenting a very broken surface.

With the exception of a single line of modern barracks, a mess-room with officers' quarters, a good house for the engineer in command, and a hospital and range of cells, the whole of the buildings were of ancient date; and among them were no less than four chapels, now appropriated as barrack-rooms and storehouses. Several of these bore the remains of profuse ornament, especially round the windows, and the winged lion occupied his usual position on the walls. It is a puzzling thing to comprehend the use of so many chapels within so small a space; but it appears that the Venetian nobility never resided far from their strongholds in those troublous times of old, when corsairs, Turkish and Algerine, cruised to ravage and plunder, and in consequence many of the opulent landholders had permanent residences within the fortress walls. The houses containing the official departments and local staff were most curiously and irregularly dispersed, and almost concealed from each other by the holes and hummocks into which the ground was broken.

The remains of splendid tanks, constructed by the engineers of Venice, and left to fall into ruin by our own, were evidence of the importance once attached to this fortress; but at present the water for the use of the scanty garrison is brought in carts at a great expense during the summer months from a spring on the hill, and is quite insufficient for their proper supply. With the exception of a few mulberry and fig trees the whole space is bare of shade, and carpeted by the rough pile of the long rank grass, with the numerous tribe of wild-flowers that never cease to variegate it. The sun, in consequence, never fails to pour his " all-potent wrath" on this devoted spot, and in the hot months the men are strictly confined to their rooms till late in the afternoon. This drawback is in some degree counterbalanced by the fresh pure mountain-air, and the absence of offensive drains, and the impure atmosphere of the town. The town barracks consisted of a tall square building, situated in a very contracted yard, enclosed by high walls, and a Greek chapel, the whole glaring with whitewash. Near to it a long barn-like building served the purpose of officers' mess-room, and a veranda at the rear overlooked a garden of orange, lemon, and oleander trees.

The men had scarcely commenced their tour of duty in Zante, when the following orders appeared in the regimental orderly-book.

GENERAL ORDER.

Corfu, May 10, 1856.

The major-general commanding cannot allow the Royal ———— Militia to leave the head-quarters of the command, without expressing to the commanding-officer, the officers, non-commissioned officers, and privates of the corps, the great satisfaction which he felt at the very regular, steady, and soldierlike manner in which it embarked this day, which he himself witnessed; it agrees with the opinion he entertains of the general discipline and good conduct of the corps, which were apparent when they arrived here, and which he has the satisfaction to think have increased and become more conspicuous since they came to this station.

R. WALPOLE,
Col. D. Q.-M. General.

REGIMENTAL ORDER.

Zante, May 26, 1856.

The commanding-officer has much pleasure in publishing the following extract from a letter rèceived from Major Daniels, with reference to the barracks lately occupied by the regiment at Corfu.

" I have no hesitation in declaring, that during the last fourteen years I have not taken over a barrack in so good a state as that of the Royal ———; everything showed that the greatest attention had been constantly paid to cleanliness and regularity."

CHAPTER XXII.

THE general situation of the town of Zante bears a considerable resemblance to that of Dover, supposing the castle-hill to represent the heights in rear of the latter town, and the highlands of Acroteri the site of the castle of Dover, but on a smaller scale, Mount Scopo at the other extremity taking the place of Shakspeare's Cliff. This disposition must be considered as referring to locality alone, Acroteri much more resembling in configuration the line of cliffs between Dover and Folkstone, while the hill of Scopo rises in a gentle slope from a succession of smaller undulations culminating in a point. Zante boasts a very good vegetable and fruit market, and the numerous fountains dispensing the clear cool waters from Scopo are a great blessing to the inhabitants. There is one large commodious street, clean, and decently paved. It runs a distance of above half-a-mile, and several old Venetian houses on each side arrest the eye by the ornate devices, carved in a handsome yellow-brown stone, that surround the windows like the setting of a jewel. A few of these are kept very clean, and in the highest state of preservation, but the majority are dingy from neglect and dirt, and their gloomy flats are the abodes of poverty and vermin. I was myself a tenant of one for a short time, and such an extraordinary conglomeration of mosaic, carved iron-work, gilded mirrors, flies and filth, I never before encountered. While there I became acquainted with a habit that prevails in Zante very conducive to early rising. At five in the morning a confused tinkling of bells in the court below proclaims that the early division of goats have arrived, and all who want milk hurry jug in hand outside their doors. Then up rush the whole flock, hop-step-and-jump, each joining in a chorus of interjectory baas, treble, contralto, and simple guttural, as announcing their age and sex. Then comes the scuffle for the milk, one holding the Nanny, a second the jug, and a third the kid, furious at beholding his own natural aliment dribbling into a stranger's delf. The operation, you may well conceive, acts as an effectual rouser.

Edibles are cheap in Zante, but the choice is very limited, and it is no fitting home for the gourmand. There is one particular fruit which is never seen in the Zante market. I allude to the currant-grape, which it is not permitted to expose for sale, on account of the temptation it would thereby hold out for depredation on the part of the peasantry. Amid piles of fruit and vegetables are seen a number of large wicker baskets, in which are confined a dozen or so of pretty-coloured and plump-looking doves, which are caught in nets, and are frequently to be purchased for a penny each, and form a great portion of the food of the shopocracy at certain seasons. Large quantities of fine turkeys are imported at certain times of the year from the coast of Greece, which, after being picked, are suspended in the butchers' shops with all the importance of a Christmas bullock, and the assistant carves off for each customer the particular slice required; so that he may return to his domestic pot with a bit of the breast, a neck, a gizzard, a thigh, a wing, a drumstick, or a parson's nose, according to his means and appetite.

From the nature of the ground on which the town of Zante is built, it is evident that the important lines of communication must run lengthwise with the shore. The intersecting streets are, with few exceptions, mere alleys, and as they near the hills in the rear assume gradually the character of a flight of steps. These lanes frequently become more contracted above by a habit of making a permanent enclosure of the whole range of upper balconies by a light frame of wood reaching to the tiles, and resembling a gigantic pigeon-hutch, and imparting a cocked-hat look to the houses. The lower portion of the hill has been much invaded by the town and small enclosed gardens, and a few vineyards diversify the lower ranges of its steep ascent, and here and there a contracted natural platform has been chosen as a shelf on which to lodge a little chapel and nest of cottages, the approach being generally the mere bed of a water-course worn in the rainy season by the floods.

Nothing is more strange to the eye of an Englishman, accustomed to the laborious neatness of his villages at home, than the odd conglomeration of cabins cuddling together that go to form a Greek hamlet. On each side a precipitous gully, in which the drainings of the flood and the foot of man and beast have worn, but by no means levelled, a winding track, a crowd of cottages, as irregularly niched as if hung on pegs, will cling at random one above another, enclosing their tiny chapel. Every hole and hummock gives site to cot or stable, while a fig-tree or two and a few cactus-plants are generally to be seen filling up the crevices. The cross-cuts that intersect the road to the castle are full of these little human nests. As I was slowly toiling up one of them, and laboriously striding from rock to rock, a little kid, the sole creature one would suppose to plan such a village, jumped merrily from a cottage-window almost on my head, and, clearing the acclivities with a succession of hops, faced me with a comic look of impudence. The peculiarity of building on an unlevelled foundation is not confined to cottages only, but may be observed in the majority of old convents and other erections of Greek origin. The hardness of the limestone rock was probably. the reason at first, and the Greeks are not a race fond of improvement.

Zante boasts no shops at which the luxuries of civilized life can be procured to any extent. In this particular it is far behind Corfu and Argostoli. I became acquainted, however, with a hairdresser, who certainly cut off more hair for sixpence than any artist I had previously employed. There are a few jewellers' shops, in which unique and intrinsically valuable articles, chiefly composed of pearls and gold, are sold by weight, no price being demanded till the scales have been referred to. There are also two establishments for the manufacture and sale of the gaily-coloured scarfs which pass under the name of Albanian, the cradle of the manufacture having been established at Yanina. The favourite one for visitors is kept by " the two old women," the name

by which this interesting pair always go in Zante.
Driving through an intricate part of the town, I
entered a tall house, and passing through a room
in which a middle-aged Greek woman was busy
at the loom, I was ushered up a steep flight of
stairs, and was soon in the presence of the "two
old women." The elder might have been seventy,
and the younger about sixty. They were evidently
sisters, and habited exactly alike in black stuff
gowns and the white calico head-dress peculiar to
elderly females in Zante. After an obeisance and
kissing my hand, they proceeded to unlock a series
of glass cases that were ranged round the apartment, and as they prided themselves on making
no abatement in price, except in the event of the
purchaser dealing largely, the process of shopping
was soon brought to a successful conclusion, and I
left the house pleased alike with my visit and my
purchases. Without any claim to great singu-
larity they were evidently originals, and their
quaint dress, clean nankeen complexions, and black
restless eyes, will ever be conjured up by my imagination in my reminiscences of Zante.

In the general arrangement of the chapels, as
far as their interior is concerned, the routine of
their ritual admits of but little distinction. In
some of the larger ones the pictures that lined the
wall were in a higher style of art than any I had

seen in Corfu, with the exception of the ceiling of the church of St Spiridion. The pictures were not confined to the delineation of Scripture subjects, but in many instances embraced the more recent events of their ecclesiastical history, especially processions and other remarkable events in the history of their Church. In the cathedral of Saint Dionysius, their patron saint, the sanctified archbishop lies within a very handsome silver coffin in a small chapel of his own on one side the altar, and a *basso relievo* engraven on the silver depicts him on his death-bed, in his robes and mitre, with his episcopal staff in his hand, and a circle of priests surrounding him. On certain occasions he emerges from his box, and makes his circuit of the town, in emulation of his brother mummy at Corfu.

At the resident's ball I was introduced to the present archbishop, a white-haired man, small in stature and bowed with age, with very keen lively eyes, and a somewhat Jewish cast of feature, but with an expression that shone with benevolence, and a kind smile and warm pressure of the hand for all, without distinction of religion or station. The eagerness with which the Greeks of all ranks pressed forward to kiss his hand, testified to the estimation in which he was held. He was described to me as a man without guile, and of unbounded kindness of heart. It would be unfair, while on this topic, to pass by without remark the Roman-catholic priest, a man advanced in years, and whose whole life appears to have been one round of Christian labour and charity. His noble devotion, during the prevalence of the cholera in the year fifty-five, will never be erased from the memory of the Zantiotes.

As I do not profess to write a history of Zante, I will not attempt a sketch of the pitch and grease wells, my most potent reason being that I never went to see them, having heard, on good authority, that it would be sheer waste of time to do so, and that the search would lead me through a very uninteresting part of the island, and that the time of year would render the sun a most formidable enemy. With regard to the grease-wells, I was told you start in a carriage, then shift to a mule, then get into a boat, and then swim; and as the swimming would have been the only part of the day's performance I should have looked forward to with any pleasure, I declined the trip altogether.

There is one spot, whence the beauty of Zante and the glory of it can be so well seen, that I must conduct the reader there before we can bid adieu to this lovely island. Climbing a flight of stone steps, under cover of a loopholed wall, we gain the bastion on the highest point of the castle, on which

floats the Union Jack, and the whole panorama of
Zante lies beneath us. The town, the bay, Scopo,
and Acroteri, have been described before; but on
one side, winding below us, shut in by lofty hills,
save where it meets a blue little bay edged with
silver, lies one of the most charming and singular
plains eye ever rested on. It would seem as if a
single angry wave might rise and resume the
watery dominion, so wondrously level does the lap
of earth appear. The almost imperceptible tide of
the Mediterranean might to all appearance have
just ebbed from it, were it not that in place of
silver sand, it is green with a carpet of currant-
vines; and chateaux with their gardens and avenues, farm buildings and cottages are sprinkled over
it, gleaming in the sun, and a maze of white roads
diverging from the hills and making for the city,
streak it like veins on the back of the hand.

This is the " Valley of Diamonds." Here, on the
lap of earth, in fragrant bunches, lie the ingots that
form the wealth of Zante. With what anxiety
does the proprietor watch the development of these
tiny delicate globules. Two years of blight had
brought poverty and despair to many a hearth;
but by sprinkling the blossom liberally with powder
of sulphur a cure became gradually effected, and
the year fifty-six promises to reward the toil of the
careful husbandman. A walk through this valley

well repays the trouble. The noble chateau of
Count Lunzi reminds the stranger of a gentleman's
seat in England; and the well-ordered estate of
Count Salamo is famous for an avenue of quince-
trees extending above a mile.

Glancing the eye immediately below the parapet
of the flag-staff bastion, it encounters a strange
wild abyss of rifted sand stretching in flakes to
the plain below, and ragged as splintered rock.
This has been left by the convulsions of a series of
earthquakes that threaten in no long time to absorb
the bastion itself. May I not be there to see!
There is yet one spot that will repay a visit. I
allude to the ruins of the palace and garden of the
late Queen of Naples. Built on the edge of a
ravine, and overlooking on one side the Valley of
the Diamonds, the crumbling walls and shattered
busts and pedestals are gradually becoming the
prey of the shrubs and creepers that were planted
to adorn them. In front descended the garden,
terrace under terrace, till the lower flights were
lost in the twilight of the narrow valley. No steps
were used in the descent, but a steep zigzag path,
running between double dwarf walls, which formed
a trough for flowers, and confined at the sides by
another wall on which vases and busts were placed
at intervals, led the way below, and must have
glowed like a visioned ladder of flowers, down

which might have tripped the footsteps of Flora when she deigned to visit earth; but now, alas! all is a tangled mass of odorous vegetation. The unpruned rose, the scarlet and white oleander, and a host of other shrubs and creepers, render the scene at once beautiful and mournful. " Oh Zante, Zante—*Fior di Levante*," says the poet, and for once he tells the literal truth. The yellow rose is here a perfect and noble flower, and to give a catalogue of the varieties of Flora's children that here attain the highest perfection would require the knowledge of a Loudon or a Paxton.

Painful would it have been had truth compelled me to declare that the Eves that wander amid this Eden of flowers and fruits had degenerated from the pristine loveliness of their sex; but the fair living roses of Zante are renowned for their charms, and I much deplore that circumstances prevented me from making many acquaintances among the aristocracy of the island; but there are many lovely faces and forms which will ever live in my memory amid the verdure and sunbeams of the " Islands of the Blest."

The peasantry are a handsome race, small in stature, but shapely and active. The women become prematurely old from hard work and exposure; but the children of both sexes are peculiarly beautiful, the eyes dark and lustrous, and the nose and lips, especially the latter, chiselled with a delicacy that reminds one of the *chef-d'œuvres* of their ancient sculptors.

Among the agreeables of a sojourn in the Grecian islands must be enumerated the facility of ranging, which enables the tourist to wander at his will throughout all the recesses of the country. The undefined and little-heeded laws of property, that exert so malign an influence over the material prosperity of the landed interest, and carry with them just sufficient weight to become an engine of oppression in the hands of a rogue, and a beacon to scare honest men from any attempt to embark capital in the improvement of the soil, stand friends to the lover of nature, and enable him to pursue without fear of hindrance, not only the bridle-roads and mountain-paths that seam the sides of the hills and meander through the valleys, but every goat-track or bed of mountain-gully that may tempt by promise of hidden beauty, or the more fallacious hope of a short cut. It is true that the majority of vineyards are enclosed by dwarf walls of dry rubble, but it is only during the seasons of the setting and ripening of the grapes that the stranger runs the risk of being molested in his passage across them; while in the open fields and never-ending groves of olive he may rove as chartered a libertine as any of nature's wildest offspring. The Greeks trust little to fence or bolt, but around each lonely cottage keep watch and ward a tribe of half-starved tall and wiry dogs resembling somewhat in appearance an underbred hound. By arming himself with a stone a man may pursue his way without fear of an attack, and soon learns to despise the annoyance; but it is better to go no farther, as every Greek cherishes his Argus, though he half-starves him, and will revenge his fall. On the coast of Albania blood for blood is the rule of vengeance, which the fierce shepherds are not slow to enforce for this offence, which many a sporting Englishman has found out to his cost. In the course of these unchecked wanderings the stranger will often find himself in the midst of an orange and lemon grove, in which, if not ashamed of himself, he may pick and eat without cost; but he will generally find a hut at no great distance, and in return for a small coin will be made welcome to eat his fill. A pedestrian, in an orange-grove on a hot day has little to envy in Mahomet's paradise.

The pasture lands in Greece soon change their garb of green for not exactly the russet, but, more correctly speaking, the nankeen mantle of autumn, or rather of summer; for before the beginning of July has commenced contracting the sun's reign, only to intensify his power, the work of preparing the Grecian hortus siccus has commenced. Beautiful is the first outburst of early April, every sod of turf bearing its own nosegay, and every patch, blue, green, and red, is tender and succulent. Then a change commences. Gradually ranker and coarser rises the herbage, and hard and tough wax the stalks, then, ere another month be past, a rough and tangled net of yellow sun-dried stubble deforms the ground and crackles under the tread. A few plants defy the hottest glare. The vine nestles over her ripening clusters without spoiling her complexion of delicate green. The cactus sends forth an array of little round yellow flowers, dotting its rhinoceros hide, and outstaring the sun.

The thistle-tribe shows a brave front, and succumbs but slowly to the blistering heat; and a peculiar species of it, which is common also in Egypt, and supposed by botanists to be the plant that was woven to form our Saviour's crown of thorns, sends forth an upright stem studded on all sides with white flowers in shape somewhat resembling the snapdragon. My favourite thistle, however, was a little upstanding, straightlaced fellow, as tough and angular as if made of wire. When the sun besets him sorest he scorns to shrink a petal, nor tries to shirk him by doubling up or covering his head with down, but simply turns bluer and bluer—not the damp, dull colour of the

New Brunswick blue nose, but a bright, cheerful, spangly blue, and as he and his friends, like jolly social fellows, are always found herding together in patches, they form a singular and very pretty variety of pattern in this carpet of nature.

One of the noisiest and most restless little fidgets, never holding his tongue, but keeping the game alive under the hottest sun, is a winged insect called the cicala. He is difficult to catch in day-time, but at eve he will occasionally indulge himself in a snooze on the grey bark of the olive-tree, which he greatly resembles in colour. In shape he is like the common fly, but is as large as an humble bee, and the moment your fingers close upon him he sets up an appeal compounded of a squall and a watchman's rattle, and without an instant to take breath prolongs it till he regains his liberty. It is difficult to feel assured that the tiny creature be-tween your finger and thumb is really and truly the author of so grievous an outcry, but only ad-vance him towards your ear, and you may make what experiment you choose on the strength of your tympanum. It is a peculiarity of this insect that he sheds his coat entire, sleeves and all, and leaves it sticking to the bark on which he last changed it; and so perfectly does it retain its shape, that its transparency alone distinguishes it from the body of its late owner, who, if he have any affection left for it, may sit and sing by it at night, and use it for an overcoat if he should feel chilly, for ought I know to the contrary.

It was in Zante that I first became witness of the primitive method of separating the corn from the ear by treading it out with cattle. A hard piece of level ground was selected, and in the centre of it was driven a stout upright post. Three horses, harnessed abreast, were fastened to this by a long cord, and a Greek lad, with whip uplifted, and a volley of shrieks and curses, set them off at a gallop. Of course they could only move in a circle, the area of which diminished in the proportion the cord wound itself round the post, till the wretched cattle, floundering among the straw, that reached to their knees, came fairly to a stand-still. They were then unloosed and their heads turned the other way, and being again attached and set in motion, the rope commenced unwinding till the horses were stopped, and so on *da capo*. A lady standing by was surprised to see us looking on with such interest. Why, said she, it is what you do at home. You thrash there with horses. True; but she had forgotten the machine.

The month of August had scarcely set in when I was made aware of the fact that the unfeathered bipeds of this island were accustomed periodically to set to building. Silently and assiduously arose a multitude of nests throughout the breadth of the land, and various as the infinite species of birds were the nests of their human imitators. Some, taking advantage of the spreading arms of an old olive-tree, would huddle together a coarse magpie kind of domicile, with a few refuse sticks, straw, and bushes. Some would make theirs crow-fashion, uncouth, strong, and heavy; while others, votaries of the titmouse, would frame it with the greatest care and taste, lacing it in pretty patterns with bamboos, hollowing fanciful windows, and even adding a veranda, while every point and angle became alive with the merry whir of little painted windmills that spun and sparkled in the sun.

As you pass along the Valley of the Diamonds, these fragile Arcadian bowers delight the eye by their quaint variety, and within them, in the stilly night, the pipe of the watcher trills merrily, and beguiles the weary hours till dawn glows on the tender vines bending under their load of clusters. Near the farm buildings, on a yard composed of dry clean earth prepared for the purpose, the gathered bunches lie blushing in purple squares, drying in the sun, like a grand carpet of state, and in the middle of each square a tiny cross, hung with the richest clusters, recalls to the mind of the reaper the God of peace and plenty. At night, at each angle of these squares, lamps of the country oil are set burning, and as the gazer looks over the valley it half persuades him that it is enchanted ground, and that the twinkling lamps are the sparkle of the diamonds.

It soon became evident that as far as the regiment was concerned it was fortunate for us that so large a portion of our foreign service had been spent at Corfu. The division of the regiment into two portions, and the difficulty of combining them on the same ground for the purpose of drill, on account of the steepness of the hill and the intense heat of the weather, could not be overcome, and rarely was it possible to get up a field-day. On the twentieth of April we had our first drill on the esplanade, and on the twenty-fourth, being the queen's birth-day, the men paraded there at noon, and fired a *feu-de-joie* in honour of the day. On the twenty-ninth a grand ball was given at the residency to celebrate the event, and the band of the regiment was in attendance. The period spent in Zante was a very uneventful one in our career. The men were much esteemed by the inhabitants for their quiet and orderly conduct, and although the certainty of arriving home too late for the harvest, in addition to their being cognizant of the departure homeward-bound of their more fortunate brothers-in-arms of the other regiments of militia, who had served a shorter time abroad, had a bad impression on the men, yet the defaulters' books of the regiment recorded nothing but the most venial offences, nor was it necessary to apply for a single district court-martial. At length, by the midnight mail of the thirteenth of August news arrived that the steamer Mauritius was in Corfu harbour, and would soon make her appearance with troops for our relief, consisting of a wing of the Sixty-eighth Regiment.

On Sunday the seventeenth, soon after dark, the lights of a large steamer were seen in the distance, and the throbbing of her engines were heard across the still waters. The outline of her tall hull became plainer and plainer in the moonlight, and at last the joyful fact was announced by the telegraph, that a steamer with troops on board was entering the harbour, and three hearty cheers resounded from the barracks in Zante, and were re-echoed from the castle. On Monday all preparations were completed, and on Tuesday the nineteenth, at two o'clock, the men fell in as clean and sober as if for the inspection of a general officer, and marched to the mole, passing on their way the companies of Her Majesty's Sixty-eighth Regiment *en route* to take up their quarters. They were conveyed, as before, by barges to the steamer's side, and found on board two companies of their old friends the Potteries, whom they had parted with at Corfu. On Tuesday at noon the steamer got under weigh, and ere the sun sank the shores of Zante had faded from our view. A fresh breeze dead ahead throughout the night thinned the next morning's breakfast-table, and redoubled our longing to set foot once more on terra firma at Malta.

At dawn on Friday the twenty-second the rocky coast of Malta appeared in sight, and at ten we steamed once again into its beautiful bay, and cast anchor beneath the spires and towers of Valetta. The health-officer boarded us as usual, and after him an amphibious shoal of youngsters paddled alongside and swarmed to the deck. At first sight they might have been set down for monkeys. Small were they, lean, and of a baboon-brown, with restless roguish eyes and prehensile toes; but their chatter reduced itself before long to a palpable lingo, and " Something for dive," " Something for dive," was the burthen of the chorus. A small coin jerked into the water, was followed like its shadow by one of these brats, and rescued from the mermaids before it had sunk below green water. A sixpence tempted one of the bigger ones to dive beneath the keel, leaping from one of the quarter-boats, and reappearing on the other side. This was our first introduction to the rising hopes of the Maltese matrons, and as each little wriggling body cut its hole through the surface with a slap like a soda-water cork, the circling green of the sparkling wave, with its spangles of pearly drops, seemed the very type of freshness and luxury, and for a moment I could almost have compounded to be Maltese or monkey to have taken part in so tempting a souse.

A smart pull in one of the green and yellow shore-boats brought us once more to the landing-place of Malta, and ascending the " nix mangiare" or " nothing to eat" stairs, a locality so named from a famous family of beggars who revelled many years on the fat of the land, by dint of swearing unceasingly from morn to eve that they had tasted nothing for sixteen days, we commenced undergoing our second roasting in the torrid streets of Valetta. Anxious to vary the scene, we looked out for a vehicle; and a pair of active horses, in a very comfortable carriage of modern build, whisked us off, a four-mile trip, to the Saint Antonio gardens, the country residence of the governor. Lofty walls enclosed a spacious square, which was traversed by two miles of paved walks at right angles to each other, their sides protected by lines of wooden trellis-work about five feet in height, and covered with luxuriant vines. The intervening spaces were crowded with fig, orange, and loquat trees, and at one end was a handsome fountain, its watery lap verdant with aquatic plants, through which flashed shoals of gold and silver fish. In the centre of this angular Eden was a circle formed of a magnificent hedge of box, and containing a collection of showy but common flowers, and on the walls of the governor's house, protected by trellis-work, were some magnificent specimens of the plumbago.

Next day, at 10 A. M., we once more got up steam, and bade a final adieu to Malta, passing, as we left the harbour, a Prussian frigate which had just put in from a cruise on the coast of Barbary, where, in quest of a few laurels to make a beginning for a future naval wreath, she had been rather roughly handled by a score or two of Riff pirates, and her commander, Prince Adelbert, was then lying seriously wounded at Gibraltar.

CHAPTER XXIII.

On the twenty-seventh we coasted along the rocky
shores of Spain, and at noon passed within a few
yards of a ninety-gun Turkish man-of-war, bowling along under studding-sails. We gave her
three hearty cheers, which were returned lustily by
the Turk. The sea was smooth, and the ladies on
deck, and we enjoyed the usual pastimes of a ship's
company under the shade of the friendly awning,
with " the blue above and the blue below," but
anything but " silence" anywhere, but chat, cigars,
and shilling novels instead, enlivened by the frequent strains of the band. Our recreations were
varied by frequent parades of all hands and feet,
cleanliness being the greatest safeguard against disease on board ship. The steersman stood elevated
on a platform of wooden lattice-work, and within
this cage-like structure the children were led to believe that a lion and six monkeys were kept in

durance, and the whir of the fan and the scrooping
of the screw below was appealed to as the cries
and roars of this too closely united family. A host
of little eager eyes were continually peering through
the holes, and little fingers thrust through and hur-
riedly withdrawn, as a thump of the screw imitated
with fearful effect the lash of the lion's tail. The
steward, however, made report of such a fearful
consumption of biscuit furtively abstracted and
dropped through the lattice, lest the lion should be
driven by stress of hunger to fall upon the monkeys, that it became necessary to dispel the delu-
sion.

At about six o'clock on the morning of the
twenty-ninth the Mauritius came to anchor in the
bay of Gibraltar; and under the shadow of its
mighty rock the Royal Blanks were once more at
rest. So long a time spent among mountains and
fortresses had perhaps somewhat dulled our appreciation of the grand and beautiful; for I must confess my first view of the famous rock a little disap-
pointed me. As is the case with Niagara, some
time is required to enable one to imbibe the full
grandeur of the sight; but before we had left the
bay I had learned to look with becoming awe on
its unparalleled concentration of all that is great
and terrible in nature and art. Having had a case
of small-pox on board we were compelled to hoist

the yellow flag, although the same disease was at
the very time prevalent in the town; but after a
morning lost in alternate hopes and fears, the sick
man was sent ashore, and at 2 P. M. we got pratique, and were soon entering the gates of the old
fortress.

In character with the antecedents of the spot we
did not step ashore without a fierce engagement,
our enemy consisting of four Gibraltar boatmen,
who modestly demanded twenty-one shillings, and
were more than doubly paid by receiving in the end
five. The language also was peculiarly appropriate to the site, which was called the Devil's
Tongue. Passing through a barrack-square with
a guard of Highlanders at the gate, we hustled
through groups of Moors, black, white, and tawny,
in flowing robes and bright turbans, Spaniards in
fringed leggings and sombreros, soldiers, sailors,
mules, goats, and donkeys, and I was soon at the
quarters of an old friend then in command of a
regiment fresh from the Crimea, who proved a
friend in need, and harnessing a splendid mule,
that had done him good service in the terrible
winter of fifty-five, to an Irish car, he drove me the
whole round of the works.

It is from the neutral ground or north side that
the rock assumes in my judgment its most imposing character. Wedge-shaped and sheer as a

precipice, it towers heavenward gaunt and weather-
stained to its fullest height, like the limbless wreck
of a shattered oak, its apex a flake of jagged rock
keen as a saw, running in an uneven ridge towards
its southern extremity. No girdle of embrasures
visible to the eye scar its rugged front of granite,
but loopholes, bored in horizontal ranges at successive elevations, mark the abiding watch of guns of
the heaviest calibre, each within its cavern hewn
from the solid rock, with its galleries of approach
in the rear, and forming one of the strongest
and most unique batteries known in the science of
war.

Below lies a wide expanse of perfectly level
sandy soil—a range of cattle-sheds and slaughter-
houses—a collection of market-gardens choke-full
of vegetables ready peppered with dust, and an
extensive cemetery crammed with tombs, many of
which are entirely covered, by way of ornament,
with a layer of large shells encrusted on a surface
of plaster. It seems somewhat out of character to
be smart over a graveyard, yet amid these stones
and shells might the editor of our old friend Bell
wander, rapt in other musings than those of Sterne
or Blair. Here 'neath this sun-dried soil should
rest the bones of Nimrod, Ward, Musters, and
other mighty hunters, while the seers of the turf,
your Pegasus, your Vates, and their imps of the

tout-tribe, would here find an appropriate resting-place at the close of their prophetic existence; for on one side, scarce a hunter's leap from conse-crated ground, stands the modest but cleanly kept edifice devoted to the comfort of the garrison fox-hounds, while, on the opposite one, the very palings are brushed by the rustling silk of the Jocks in all the excitement of the " run in " for garrison cups and stakes, beneath the smiles and plaudits of the garrison belles in the grand stand opposite. It is evident the serious people must contrive never to die during the race-week. Such and so various are the monuments with which John Bull has here covered the surface of his own modicum of ground. Pass onward, and your way lies through a line of red-coated sentries, and you tread the dreary space of sandy soil denominated the neutral ground, with its crop of Spanish beggars, Spanish hucksters, and the mouldering remains of Spanish prowess in the shape of the nearly obliterated lines and ruined forts that once in vain spent their storm of shot and shell during the ever-memorable siege.

Next come a range of white stone sentry-boxes and guard of Spanish soldiers in white trousers and blue coatees, with red facings and green shoulder-knots, all of French cut, and a group of Douaniers actively engaged in rummaging the panniers of numerous donkeys on their way to the fortress with their loads of fruit and vegetables. Pass the sentry-boxes, and you are in veritable Spain, on a bad dusty road with nothing to see on either side, and quite ready to turn back and revisit the realms of Queen Victoria.

A chat with my friend on our return enlightened me a little as regards the military marvels of the place. Bowling smoothly over a complex concatenation of moats and bridges, I was startled at being suddenly informed, that at a wink from the governor I might be blown incontinently sky-high, and were I to fall in the moat, and life by any miracle left within me, I should be received at the bottom into such a satanic system of pits, stakes, hooks, and fiendish contrivances, that not a hair of my head would ever reappear on the surface.

With the exception of an old Moorish castle, there is little to interest in the town itself, which lies at the foot of the rock in two divisions, joined by about a mile of land on which something will grow, and which is laid out accordingly in esplanades, parades, botanical gardens, and private villas. All the soil of Her Majesty's dominions in this territory seems to. have been sedulously scraped together on this spot, and a rustico-military bit of landscape gardening on the old model is the result. A powerful battery, masked by turf and roses, and named appropriately "the snake in the grass," peers, itself invisible, over this bit of Eden, and granite governors, and heroes in bronze and brass, look calmly dignified across the levelled lawn, or point menacingly with their batons at beds of geraniums. The southern extremity of the town, abutting on the ledge of rock that cleaves the sea, leaving on one side the waters of the Straits and on the other those of the Mediterranean, and submerged and lashed by the billows of both " when the stormy winds do blow," is more exclusively military in its aspect, and is replete with all those works in brick and stone, scarping, grubbing, banking, and ditching, amid which it is the fate of heroes to breathe and have their being. Among the rest is a small square bomb-proof barrack sunk into the rock, and named the Bear-pit from its exact resemblance to a certain cavernous place of abode in the Regent's Park. Here, however, are caged certain subalterns whose prospects, as far as the landscape goes, appear to differ but little from those of their zoological rivals, minus the pole and buns.

Little did we think, when we first cast anchor in this harbour, what a host of future troubles were destined to spring from our detention here. A fine clipper ship, the Tudor, of twelve hundred tons, lay near us, and on board her were a motley and swarthy crowd, the heroes that composed the three regiments of the Italian Legion. Attired in their respective uniforms of red, blue, and grey, by which the first, second, and rifle regiments were distinguished, they became to us a source of great interest, more especially as rumour informed us that it was not without good cause that she lay so snugly moored under the fortress guns; for a serious attempt at mutiny and seizure of the ship for the purpose of making a descent on the coast of Sicily, while in sight of it on their passage from Malta, had only been frustrated by the prompt and fortunately bloodless defeat of an attack on the English officers in command by certain of their Italian comrades. This soon proved to be a fact, for an officer, in close arrest, was put on board of us for conveyance to England for trial by court-martial. He was a lithe, soldier-like, swarthy man, somewhat under the middle size, with the true Italian cast of countenance. At first, doubtful of his reception among us, he assumed a fierce and defiant air; but as we thought it no business of ours to assume the high moral tone over a poor devil who had committed his crime within sight of the prison in which one of his brothers had died and another was then in close confinement, he became reconciled to his situation, and behaved as a quiet gentlemanly man. He was especially a favourite with the children, for whom he was constantly inventing puzzles, or otherwise amusing them. Captain Angera had played a conspicuous part in the troubles of Italy. At Plymouth we saw the last of him on his way to the citadel under charge of a guard. His last act on board was to express his thanks for the kindness he had met with from us.

This incident heightened the melodramatic effect of the scene we watched at nightfall, when by the glare of the ship's lights their dusky figures flitted indistinctly about the deck, while a chorus of wild songs, the lays of revolutionary Italy, rose musically on the still night-air, and a storm of fierce exulting shouts broke forth savagely at the close.

We had not been long in the bay when we received, with a certain degree of pride, a visit from a boat of Her Majesty's steamer Prometheus. To be taken such notice of by swells raised us not a little in our own opinion, and when we found they brought a message intimating the desire of Captain Hoare to hold colloquy with our skipper, we were at a loss to estimate duly the honours that were probably in store for us. The return of our skipper was earnestly watched for, and when at length he hove within hail, the lengthened aspect of his visage told sensibly on our spirits. His tale, on reaching the deck, was short and not sweet. We were simply required by the gallant commander to do the work for which he was expressly stationed in port, and as our engines had only broken down four times on our passage from Zante, it was reckoned but just and proper that we should tow the Tudor home, and not lose sight of her till she should be safe at Plymouth. Disheartening as the announcement was, we had then no idea of the troublous times we were doomed to pass with our future consort.

At early dawn on the thirtieth we pulled ashore for a last look at Gibraltar, and were soon in mid-market, which is held close to the landing-place. Spaniards of both sexes driving donkeys and mules laden with panniers full of magnificent fruit and vegetables, were discharging their stores on the slabs, where they were arranged in tempting order fresh and clean by the stall-keepers. All the prime favourites of the British *hortus culinarius* seemed well represented here, and even " our butcher," in his John Bullockest of moods, might have deigned to smile on the beef, minus as it was of oil-cake and stall-feeding. Red mullet, fresh and rosy as the dawn, gigantic lobsters, and dusky, grim rock-cod, did the honours of the fishmarket. A shave by a Spanish barber, that marvel of soap and steel, and unrivalled as a class among the artists of their fraternity, whose razors charm the

stubbiest of chins with a titillation as soft as the
fingers of Anna Matilda, brought us to the close
of our shore-leave, and after a leap into the sea
which made us shiver, accustomed as we had been
to the tepid waters that lave the shores of Corfu,
we returned to our boat, attended by a shoal of
market-boys, pressing on us huge baskets of Fron-
tignac grapes, basket and all, for a shilling. I
offer the reader no excuse for not dwelling longer
on the wonders of this famous rock. I am the
ninety-ninth at least of the scribblers to whom this
innocent stone-giant has been the unconscious subject of blarney or discussion. His age—his height
—his breadth—his shape—his colour, have been
described and squabbled over *ad nauseam*. They
have handled his mighty torso, and prosed over
his deeds, as though he had been Ben Caunt or
the Slasher. They have burnt blue lights in his
bowels, and shuddered as they peered down his
cavernous jaws with their rows of stalactite teeth.
They have scraped off his lichens, and torn away
his little stock of botany with a sneer. They have
sniffed his powder and d——d his east wind, vili-
fied his apes, and one boasts of having ridden *en
cheval* on his back; but unmoved the grand old
fellow rests, impervious to their attacks, and shall
do so till the rocks melt, and then indeed will
there be a precious fusion of Christian, Jew, and

Turk, salt junk, sea biscuit, soldiers, sailors, governors, apes, and aides-de-camp.

Our first near acquaintance with the Tudor began with a weary hour spent in backing and manœuvring to get a fair hold, and the stout hawser strained and stretched till it parted with a snap like a pistol-shot. Again came a Babel of orders and directions through a brace of speaking-trumpets, and once more the hawser tightened, and away it went again with a crack and a curse; and that the injury under which we were smarting should not want a spice of insult to ram it well home, at this very juncture the abominable Prometheus squibbed off one of her guns, and ran up the signal, " What are you waiting for." At length we slowly sneaked out of harbour, dragging the unlucky Tudor wearily at our stern.

CHAPTER XXIV.

OUR course now lay within sight of shore, and we passed close to Cape St Vincent with its fortifications and lighthouse, and next day we were coasting the shores of Portugal, and were treated to a clear view up the Tagus, with Lisbon and Cintra in the distance, and the shipping in the port below them. The monotony of the voyage became now hourly relieved by some accident or other happening to the hawsers, and no brace of dogs newly coupled gave their owners more annoyance than the Tudor and Mauritius. On the third of September the engine broke down, and on the fourth, at midnight, the same thing occurred again, and we narrowly escaped the peril of being run into by the ship in tow. At length she was cut adrift, and we agreed to sail in company. A board composed of an equal number of the captains of the two regiments was now assembled, and the debate on the great cable question ended by a protest being forwarded to the skipper deprecating the continuance of our ominous conjunction with the Tudor, notwithstanding which she was again taken into tow, and on the fifth, being short of water, we made for the port of Vigo, and reached the entrance between two lofty rocks just before sunset. We sailed up a magnificent estuary, and on each side of us hills of vivid green, with large houses square and white, groves of pine, and cultivated fields separated by hedges into unequal chequers, reminded us of the woodland heights and rich pastures of Devon. Seldom had we seen a more beautiful bay. In the far horizon hill seemed rising over hill, the tints of distance robing each alternate range in hues of successive and still mellowing colour, while partially veiled by the burnished form of a watch-tower at the entrance of the bay, the setting sun lit up the foamy breakers, and threw its level rays along the swelling lines of the shore. Sloping from an abrupt hill to the sea-beach, and under ward of an ancient castle, with moat and drawbridge still entire, the white, green, and yellow houses of the town of Vigo lay in picturesque confusion. A hill, on the summit of which a grove of lofty pines shone forth like lace-work against the clear sky, stood sentry on the left, and advanced an avenue of noble trees to meet

the town. Two Dutch merchantmen, quaint and
heavy, and of strange rig, with a variety of craft
from England and America, and not a few with
the flaunting flag of Spain at the mizzen, lay at
anchor, and further inland, half concealed by a
bend in the estuary, the masts of a whole fleet of
small craft rose at the foot of some town or village
of large size. Early next morning a roomy heavy
boat with yellow awning, and the imperial flag of
Spain at her stern, came alongside, and our captain
having provided himself with a clean bill of health,
we were at once admitted to pratique, and the
British consul came on board and promised his assistance in procuring coal and water.

The Spanish commandant behaved with great
attention and courtesy, and gave orders that every
consideration should be paid to the officers who
might come ashore, and facilities be afforded them
of inspecting the town and barracks. In the evening he came on board, accompanied by his staff.
Their dress and demeanour were soldierlike, and
their appearance led us to expect that we should
find the garrison in good order, which proved to
be the case, for a cleaner or smarter body of little
swarthy fellows I have seldom seen. They seemed
well adapted for skirmishing or guerilla warfare,
but to be deficient in weight and muscle. I should
consider them physically incapable of standing the

charge of any British regiment. The shoulder to
shoulder rush that clears a rampart or sweeps a
plateau must be the work of broader chests and
brawnier limbs than theirs. Having obtained permission to land, I put off in a ship's boat, and
ascending a flight of broad stone steps at the
extremity of an artificial mole, stood on the soil of
Galicia. I had no time to muse or grow poetical
on Roncesvalles or the Cid, or any of the phases
of Spanish chivalry from Don Quixote to Sancho
Panza, for I was speedily surrounded by crowds of
fruit-venders and beggars, the latter all blindness,
lameness, soreness, and distortions, a most remarkable fact, considering the diligence of Spanish
saints in working miracles. I don't see the good
of getting a wink or even a tear from the smartest
of Madonnas if she won't help a man at such
pinches as these. Every request on the part of
these worthies commenced with " I say," and then
sheered off into gibberish; but the hucksters got
as far as " I say buy," and a chorus of " I say, I
say," followed us wherever we went. I discovered
without difficulty the Lion d'Or, the hotel to which
I had been recommended by the English consul,
and ascending a flight of stone steps entered a range
of passages, among which I soon became entangled,
as no one appeared to direct or receive me. At
length by dint of stumbling against several doors

with a seasonable clatter, it seemed to strike some one that there was a stranger about the house, and that the nuisance of his blindfold blunderings might be somewhat abated if he was informed whereinto to betake himself. A keenish-looking lad, not unlike an English waiter pared down and coloured olive, at last overtook me and showed me into a room, which was clean and of tolerable size, with a few flashy coloured prints, and an old mirror in a tarnished gold frame as ornaments. With some difficulty I made him understand that I wished to taste the wine of the country, and an execrable black compound soon quenched all further thirst on that head. An attempt at a later period to get dinner, although honoured on that occasion by an audience with the landlord himself, terminated in great obscurity, and when no dinner made its appearance we felt rather relieved than not, having approximated through a series of disappointments to the blessed state of him who expects nothing. I must here dedicate a few words to the person of my worthy landlord, especially as he was the type of the majority of his station whom we encountered in our wanderings about the town. He was small and meagre, closely shaved, and with a sinister supercilious expression. He had a shocking bad hat, which seemed glued to his head, and a seedy suit that might have been bought in the Minories.

A more unpicturesque-looking bad character could scarcely be imagined. In him and all the rest of his sex in Vigo, we looked in vain for the fierce whiskered Don that struts his ten minutes with such éclat on the boards of our minor theatres. An affectation of sneering us down seemed to pervade the population in general, and with the exception of the keeper of a shop of bijouterie of whom we bought some fans, and the bootmakers of whom we purchased largely, they seemed scarcely sufficiently aware of our presence to offer their goods. We discovered a kind of café in which we assuaged our hunger on good pastry washed down with excellent chocolate, and we carried on board a stock of thin circular wooden boxes containing a kind of cheese made of cherries, which we all highly approved of. We made an abortive attempt to hire a carriage for a ride into the country, for though they affected to send for one, we waited in vain for its arrival. We gained thereby a piece of information very characteristic of the people we were among, viz., that there was only one road, that to Madrid, on which a carriage could travel, and yet Vigo is one of the principal ports of Spain.

The part of Vigo most worth seeing, and in which was collected a congress of its diverse population, was the large central square and market-place. Along two sides of it ran a covered way under arches, similar, though on a much smaller scale, to that of Covent Garden. The houses of various height and character were all neat, and well built of a light-coloured stone. Their distinctive peculiarity consisted of a range of light balconies of ironwork painted green, and studded with knobs of brass brightly polished. Beneath the arches were some of the principal shops, and the whole area of the square was covered with groups of peasantry, squatting on the ground in charge of their goods, the usual medley of poultry, fruit, and vegetables. Dried pease and haricot beans seemed a favourite article of consumption. At one place a fierce quarrel was raging between a sombre-looking, brown old man, who seemed used to it, and a couple of buxom market-girls whose basket of beans he had upset. It ended, however, in words, and we had no opportunity of witnessing the knife-work that so constantly attends the finale of Spanish quarrels. This said knife is a most abominable instrument, and differs *in toto* from the equally brutal bowie-knife of America. A small portion of the handle is made of buckhorn, to which is appended a long taper curved piece of brass, ending in a blunt point, and imparting to the implement the shape of a half-moon. After being instructed in the art of opening it, which a

stranger cannot comprehend at first, he finds that
the blade, which is fastened firmly to its place with
a spring, is long and keen, terminating in a point
as sharp as a lancet, and from its peculiar shape
almost useless for any other purpose than that of
manslaughter. The mode of using it consists in
holding it tightly between the thumb and second
finger, the forefinger pressing the tapering point of
brass. It is then hurled forward like a dart, and
if the aim is correct, the sooner one party absconds
and the other makes his confession the better.
We had here an opportunity of studying the characteristics of the female population of the lower
orders, and they seemed very superior in their
physical conformation to their lords and masters.
Their figures were broad and muscular, their eyes
good, and their features marked and expressive.
I cannot call them pretty, the accuracy of the historian interfering with the gallantry of the militiaman, but they possessed the healthy cheery hue
which is beauty's best substitute. Their dark hair
was fastened neatly at the back of the head, to
which it formed the only covering. A sturdy but
well-shaped foot, guiltless of shoe or stocking,
protruded from beneath a somewhat short skirt of
blue linsey-woolsey, and an apron of some contrasting colour descended to an equal length in front.
A cloak of bright scarlet, with a broad edging of

black and a hood depending behind, completed the costume, and imparted a jaunty, gipsy air quite refreshing. Their great general resemblance in contour and feature to the women of the west of Ireland could not fail to strike any man who had sojourned in the wilds of Connamara, or sipped the forbidden mountain-dew in the rugged old town of Galway with its " Spanish square," its Claddach teeming with the wild reckless fisher-horde with their legends of Spanish colonies and Spanish gold. Another little circumstance appealed loudly to my recollections of Paddy's land. A small lean pig of fresh complexion and scarcely a shade of hair, located uncomfortably beneath the bony arm of a gaunt old peasant, like a filbert in a pair of crackers, kept up vigorously, in spite of his diminutive proportions, the hereditary larum of his race, a fact partially accounted for by the peculiarity inherent in the old fellow of dozing off, and waking up with a start and a grip, pressing his captive fondly, and churning his jaws as if mentally enjoying the crackling. Exposed along a wall for sale on coarse strips of paper, headed by hideous wood-cuts such as adorned our street songs some fifty years ago, were ranged the ballad literature of Spain. Murder, robbery, and suicide, seemed the unvarying subject of song, and in one instance a kind of triangular duel seemed in progress, presided over by a young lady playing a guitar.

Next day, being Sunday, our vessel remained in harbour, and we landed early, bent upon a stroll into the country. We passed through the avenue of black poplars, which we had seen from aboard, and found the suburbs much cleaner and wearing a much more English look than we had expected. Numerous cabarets stood invitingly open, and at the door of one of them a black-eyed Senorita proclaimed her knowledge of our tongue and taste by smirking blandly and exclaiming, "I say, buy some rum." The road we found most excellent, and large neatly squared heaps of broken stone *à la* M'Adam, and apparently of that superlative kind known at home as Bristol, lined the sides of it. Neat cottages within luxuriant gardens occurred at intervals, and close to each, but detached, was a small granary, always very neat and clean, and in some instances made very pretty with paint and ornament. Few were without pigeon-hutches, shaped as generally seen in England, and the fluttering of the birds gave a lively and domestic character to the homestead. We trudged along some miles, the road winding among hills monotonous in their green beauty. Vegetation seemed luxuriant, and combined the tropical and European productions of field and grove. Pease, beans, maize, potatoes, and barley, abounded. The evergreen oak, the chestnut with its knobs of bristly fruit, noble pines, and plots of weeping willows, formed the green waving garments of this favoured land, and around a small pool, the reservoir of an irrigating stream, a circle of lithe bamboos kept guard against the sun.

As we returned into town the bells of the cathedral were chiming for mass, and a motley crowd of market-women with their red cloaks and bare feet, mingled with plump senoras and elegant senoritas in their graceful mantillas, with the everlasting fan quivering in their fingers like the tail of a bird. We entered the cathedral, which was fast becoming crowded, and found it a gloomy but handsome structure, with less gaudiness about it than is generally displayed on the walls of similar edifices on the Continent. Within the altar-rails was a black semicircle, one-half of which was composed of nuns, and the other half of the male members of some religious order. The service not having yet commenced, they observed a deep silence; but the solemnity of the scene was suddenly broken by a shrill and most irreverent yelp, and forth from beneath the petticoats of a very fat old nun issued one of those lean, weasen, half-skinned looking mongrels called Italian greyhounds. Leisurely crossing the front of the altar, he made a sniff at the toe of one of the friars, on which being received with a jerk he retreated with another yelp, and an attempt at his capture by the nuns proving unsuccessful, each as she made her grab and regained her equilibrium, merely succeeding in evoking a snap and a snarl, the slippery little wretch glided through their fat fingers like an eel, and at last posted himself in triumph in front of the altar. His final expulsion, whether by bell, book, or candle, I did not stop to contemplate, for finding the space was becoming too contracted for the increasing stream of worshippers, I withdrew, as my presence under such circumstances was clearly an intrusion. On returning to the ship we found all in preparation for departure. A crowd of bumboats surrounded the vessel with their stores of apples, bread, and dried figs in odd-looking baskets woven from rushes, and exactly resembling church-hassocks. Oysters, too, were marvellously good and very cheap, and whole tubsful were soon arranged on both sides of the deck, and the strong-wristed, knife in hand, ejected them with a wrench from their snug holdings with as little compunction as though they had been Irish cottiers. Their revenge, however, was prompt and searching. Disasters, that cannot appear in print, spread horror and confusion that very night throughout the saloon. Next day the gradations of oyster-eating could be divined to a certainty, from the trifler in shell-fish who had but a smack of copper on his lips, to the gourmand whose interior economy felt sheathed in that mineral. In vain all protested there was an R in the month. No R can surely exist in a Spanish September. The reason alleged for this dirty behaviour on the part of the oysters, was a low and vicious habit they had acquired of sticking to the copper-bearing rocks with which their habitations are paved, a habit the less excusable, from the fact that in these same diggings lie millions of bright doubloons, and ingots of gold and silver, thrown in despair from the South American galleons when the fiery Blake was encompassing them with sword and flame in the palmy days of Queen Bess. He kept the poor Vigo citizens in an uproar from fifteen hundred and eighty-five to eighty-nine, and played Gomorrah with their town on more occasions than one. Lord Cobham followed suit in seventeen hundred and nineteen, and took the town with little opposition.

The old cable nuisance now commenced afresh, and at three o'clock we slowly steamed our way out of the magnificent harbour, and after enduring the disagreeables of a heavy ground-swell, had the satisfaction of seeing the light off Cape Finisterre before turning in. Next morning the decks were dripping, and we encountered the novelty of a whole day's rain; and at night, what was no novelty at all, the complete break-down of the engine, and narrow escape of being run down by the Tudor at dead of night. They managed to cast her off just in time, and she went her own way, disappearing rapidly in the darkness, and taking with her the earnest prayers of every soul on board that we might never see her again. The majority of us would have made friends with the Flying Dutchman in preference.

CHAPTER XXV.

THE engine being now quiescent, we got up studding-sails, and, aided by a spanking breeze, were
soon within the latitude of the Bay of Biscay. Our
joy, however, was not fated to endure long, for on
waking next morning we found the wind dead
ahead, and the ship steering direct for New York.
" There we lay all the day in the Bay of Biscay, oh,"
and the next day the same, and the same the day
after, and we were now with but two days' water
on board, making no port, and out of the track of
vessels. At this juncture, when the visages of all
concerned began to turn white, blue, black, or red,
according to their constitutions, the very core of our
hearts warmed at the sight of a steamer speeding
along on the distant horizon. We showed signals
of distress by hoisting a Union Jack upside down
at the mizzen, and dipping it at intervals in the sea.
For some time our fate was dubious, but at last, to

our inexpressible delight, she put about, and in half an hour was within hail. She proved to be the collier screw steamer Stirling, bound from Brest to Newport, a Glasgow vessel like our own, and partly owned by the same company. A little persuasion, and the payment of a round sum, induced her to take us in tow, and after the usual hawser fracas, during which the first snapped as usual, our crippled craft once more progressed, slowly but surely, towards Plymouth. The next day we sighted the entrance of that far-famed harbour, and, I am sorry to say, experienced a wicked spice of satisfaction in watching the unlucky Tudor sadly baffled by the wind, and struggling hard to tack in. We next played the poor Stirling a hawser trick, entangling it playfully round her screw, and left her in the lurch, with her whole crew hard at work on it, and had ocular proof that few predicaments are more deplorable than a steamer so unpleasantly tied by the tail.

Once again at anchor on British waters, and within reach of Her Majesty's dockyard, the day was spent in getting the machinery patched up, and at eleven o'clock next day, after hearing once more the church-chimes of our native land, we were towed out of harbour, and at the same hour next morning came to anchor at Spithead. The men now agreed to forget all troubles and hardships, and

T

as they recognised the old localities and landmarks on Southsea Common, the joke and tale went merrily round, and in a short time two steam-tugs came to escort us, and each taking an arm, as it were, (I am sorry to say our two friends smoked intolerably), conducted us into the inner harbour, the beach, the balconies, and lines being crowded with spectators, old friends cheering and waving flags and handkerchiefs, and we were once more made fast to the old jetty, and a crowd of old recollections came across us, as we watched the sentries at their monotonous duties, and thought of the olden time.

Next morning, at early dawn, the note of preparation sounded, and with their band at their head the old regiment marched once more through the streets of Portsea, and were soon stowed away in railway carriages, and, preceded by the friends of the Potteries, started *en route* for home. Everything now wore the appearance of health and happiness. The very engine-whistle sounded like sweet music. The ploughmen, as the trains passed, stopped their teams and waved their hats, and when at last the noble spire of our county cathedral hove in sight, a general cheer broke from our lips, the men leaped eagerly from the carriages, and many a hand was stretched through the railings to meet the friendly grasp of brother, son, or sweetheart. Once more the curb of discipline was drawn tight by a firm hand. The men fell in, and stood silent and motionless, while the band collected their instruments and ranged themselves at the head. It was a proud and exciting moment for all. The big drum never looked so big. The drum-major's bearskin cap seemed swollen with pride, and his scarlet feather shone as from inflammation. At length the word was given. The voice of the big drum burst forth at a whack which would have killed an alderman, and with colours flying the regiment marched through the well-known streets, drew up in the market-square, and amid the cheers of their friends and the music of the church-bells, the men were dismissed to their billets. At dawn next morning the warning bugles went the round of the streets, and within an hour the railway was again whirling its freight of red-coats through their native county, the stations on each side crowded with friends and relatives, and ere mid-day the regiment left the cars, and formed for their last march to the old town, the scene of the toils and frolics of their earliest trainings.

Seven miles through a rich dairy district, interspersed with woodland, were soon accomplished, although the month on board ship had told visibly on the condition of the men, and their feet had become swollen by standing on the wet decks. As they neared the goal that terminated their toil and travel, the evidences of their welcome home became thicker and thicker. At first a few mounted people met us, and after a brief parley spurred back. Then group by group a crowd of pedestrians joined our march, the gentler sex predominating, till the road was one scene of hubbub, and before we had entered the outskirts of the town a halt was called, in the vain hope of extricating the ranks from the pressure of the people. At length the band struck up, and, as well as circumstances would admit of, the men marched into the market-place, passing on each side a line of banners, with mottoes telling of " auld lang syne," and a hearty welcome home, while the windows were festooned with wreaths of flowers and garnished with pretty girls. On the left was drawn up the depôt of the regiment, which presented arms as we passed, and with as much speed as was compatible with the confusion consequent on an overwhelming charge of a motley host of friendly bumpkins of every age and sex, the men were paid and dismissed.

Having traced the wanderings of my old regiment by sea and land, and restored them to their homes, their labours and mine are fast drawing to a close. We were the second regiment to embark for foreign service and the last but one to return, having remained abroad for a longer period than any other militia regiment.

On Friday the nineteenth the Royal Blanks sallied
forth for the last time to their old drill-field in all
the pomp and circumstance of war, and marched
round in review order before their colonel, who subsequently addressed to them his thanks in the most
gratifying terms for their conduct, and invited them to
a dinner in the market-house at his own expense.

Accordingly, on the following Monday the long
area of the town-hall was crowded with tables
groaning under the weight of the noble quarterings
of the ox, sown with plum-puddings and supported
with pots of beer. The whole corps of officers made
a point of being present, and a toast or two, all beer
and pith, and a kind farewell-address from the
colonel, closed the proceedings with a round of ap-
plause.

I will not so libel my country's beer as to state
that it was not more potent in its effects than Zante
wine. In fact for a day or so the equilibrium of
the regiment was somewhat out of poise. There
was a pot to be drained in memory of foreign heat,
and another as an antidote to present cold. The
glories of the past, the red-coat reminiscences, and
the smock-frock *in prospectu*, the sword and the
pruning-hook, demanded their share of enthusiasm
which one fluid alone could cool or quench. A
little good advice from the officers soon checked all
disposition to license, and no quarrelling or fight-

ing, no complaining in the streets from police or civilians, marred the satisfaction with which the officers took a final farewell of their humble companions in arms. On the morning of Monday the twenty-ninth of September eighteen hundred and fifty-six, the final settlement with the corps took place. An average of about two pounds remained to be paid over to every militiaman, and in a few hours a body of men, who for above two years had formed a compact mass, cemented by the strong bond of military discipline, dispersed, each a well-trained soldier, and not a less useful citizen, to the four corners of the county, the future *vivâ voce* chroniclers of the deeds and adventures of the Royal Blanks.

CHAPTER XXVI.

I now close my narrative, throughout which I feel conscious of having done my best to be a truthful historian, however much I may have failed in proving myself an entertaining one, by the production of two official letters, one addressed to the officer commanding the regiment, and the other, which is of more general interest, to the Lord-lieutenant of the county ; and returning my best thanks to those who have had the patience to follow me through so many pages, I respectfully bid my readers farewell.

Paris, 27th September 1856.

My Lord,

I very much regret my absence when your regiment landed at Portsmouth, particularly as it was the last of the militia corps in my own district.

The Royal —— having been so little under my

command, and landed and disbanded during my absence, I cannot well say anything in orders in the way of a farewell, and I must therefore express in this more private form my very high opinion of the corps.

No regiment of militia commenced better than the Royal ———. Its composition was excellent, and even from the little I was enabled to see of the corps, it was evident its interior economy was wonderfully good for the then so newly formed one. Of the regiment when abroad I can of course only speak from report, which, however, has been most favourable; but of the depôt I may say, that no corps or detachment could have given less trouble. Upon the only occasion when I could get away to D———, I found everything in the best possible order, and the conduct of the men has been good throughout.

May I beg of your Lordship to make known to the Royal ——— my feelings towards the regiment as above embodied.

I have the honour to be,

MY LORD,

Your obedient servant,

H. W. BRETON,
Major-General.

House of Commons,
May 1856.

MY LORD MARQUESS,

In obedience to an order of the House, I have the honour to transmit to your Lordship the enclosed resolutions, which were agreed to unanimously by this House 8th of May last.

I have to request your Lordship to communicate these gratifying expressions of the thanks and approbation of the House of Commons to the officers, non-commissioned officers, and men of the distintinguished corps of Royal ——, which have been embodied during the course of the late war.

I have the honour to be,
MY LORD MARQUESS,
Your Lordship's obedient servant,
C. S. LEFEVRE.

House of Commons,
Jovis, 8 *die Maii* 1856.

Resolved, *nemine contradicente,*

That the thanks of the House be given to the officers of the service corps of militia which have been embodied in Great Britain and Ireland during the course of the war, for the zealous and meritorious services which they have rendered to their Queen and Country, at home and abroad.

U

Resolved, *nemine contradicente,*

That this House doth highly approve and acknowledge the services at home and abroad of the non-commissioned officers and men of the several corps of militia which have been embodied in Great Britain and Ireland during the course of the war, and that the same be communicated to them by the colonels or commissioned officers of the several corps, who are desired to thank them for their meritorious conduct.

Ordered,

That Mr Speaker do signify the said resolutions respecting the militia by letters to Her Majesty's Lieutenant of each county, riding, and place in Great Britain, and to His Excellency the Lord-lieutenant of that part of the United Kingdom called Ireland.

No. 669.

GENERAL ORDER.

Horse Guards, 9th June 1856.

The militia forces having been directed to be disembodied, the Field-marshal Commanding-in-chief, previously to their return to their homes, desires to offer to the officers, non-commissioned officers, and men, his best acknowledgments for the zeal and discipline which they have shown during the whole period of their service. They have not only performed every duty which fell to their share with the cheerful obedience of good soldiers, but they have in large numbers gallantly volunteered into the line at the most critical period of the war, and by thus reinforcing the British army before Sebastopol, have essentially contributed to its success.

Several militia regiments volunteered their services for the garrisons of the Mediterranean. The offer of ten regiments was accepted, thereby liberating an equal number of regiments of the line to proceed to the Crimea.

The Queen has been graciously pleased to mark her sense of these valuable services by signifying her commands through the Secretary of State for War, that the following militia regiments, which volunteered their services abroad, be permitted to bear the word " Mediterranean" on their colours : viz.

Royal Berkshire.
East Kent.
1st Royal Lancashire.
3d Royal Lancashire.
3d Royal Westminster, Middlesex.
Northampton.
Oxford.
1st King's Own, Stafford.
Royal Wiltshire.
2d West York.

The Field-marshal Commanding-in-chief congratulates these regiments on the distinction thus awarded to them by Her Majesty.

The Field-marshal has received constant reports from general officers at home and abroad, of the excellent state of discipline of the militia regiments generally ; and at this moment of their returning to their homes, he desires to express to the officers, non-commissioned officers, and private soldiers of every regiment embodied during the war, his thanks for their good conduct, and his best wishes for their welfare and happiness.

By command of the Right Honourable
Field-marshal Viscount HARDINGE,
Commanding-in-chief,
G. A. WETHERALL,
Adjutant-general.

19 AU 57

THE END.

EDINBURGH :
PRINTED BY OLIVER AND BOYD,
TWEEDDALE COURT.

65, *Cornhill, London,*
August, 1857.

NEW AND STANDARD WORKS

PUBLISHED BY

SMITH, ELDER AND CO.

NEW PUBLICATIONS.

I.

The Autobiography of Lutfullah, a

Mohamedan Gentleman, with an Account of his Visit to England. Edited by E. B. EASTWICK, Esq.

Post 8vo, price 10s. 6d., cloth.

"We have read this book with wonder and delight. Memoirs of a live Moslem gentleman are a novelty in our letters. . . . . Lutfullah's story will aid, in its degree, to some sort of understanding of the Indian insurrection."— *Athenæum.*

II.

Victoria, and the Australian Gold

Mines, in 1857; with Notes on the Overland Route. By WILLIAM WESTGARTH.

Post 8vo, with Maps, price 10s. 6d., cloth.

III.

The Sea Officer's Manual; Being a

Compendium of the Duties of a Commander; First, Second, Third, and Fourth Officer; Officer of the Watch; and Midshipman in the Mercantile Navy. By CAPTAIN A. PARISH, of the East India Merchant Service.

Small Post 8vo, price 5s. cloth.

IV.

Tiger Shooting in India. By LIEUTENANT

WILLIAM RICE, 25th Bombay N. I.

Super Royal 8vo. With Twelve Plates in Chroma-lithography.

(Nearly ready.)

V.

The Principles of Agriculture. By P.

LOVELL PHILLIPS, M.D.

Demy 8vo. *(Just ready.)*

VI.

Willie's Rest: a Sunday Story. By the

Author of "Round the Fire," &c.

Square 16mo, with Cuts.

NEW PUBLICATIONS—*continued.*

VII.

The Life of Charlotte Brontë. Author of "JANE EYRE," "SHIRLEY," "VILLETTE," &c. By MRS. GASKELL, Author of "Mary Barton," "Ruth," "North and South," &c.

Third Edition, Revised, Two Volumes, Post 8vo, with a Portrait of Miss Brontë and a View of Haworth Church and Parsonage. Price 24s. cloth.

"We regard the record as a monument of courage and endurance, of suffering and triumph . . . . All the secrets of the literary workmanship of the authoress of 'Jane Eyre' are unfolded in the course of this extraordinary narrative."—*Times.*

"By all this book will be read with interest. . . . Mrs. Gaskell has produced one of the best biographies of a woman by a woman which we can recall to mind."—*Athenæum.*

"Thoroughly well and artistically has the work been accomplished; an informing method presides over the whole; every circumstance has a direct bearing on the main object of painting, vigorously and accurately, a real picture of the woman as she was."—*Daily News.*

"The profound pathos, the tragic interest of this book, lies in the terrible struggle that life was to a woman endowed with Charlotte Brontë's conscientiousness, affection for her family, and literary ambition, and continually curbed and thrown back by physical wretchedness. Its moral is, the unconquerable strength of genius and goodness."—*Spectator.*

"Mrs. Gaskell's 'Life of Charlotte Brontë' has placed her on a level with the best biographers of any country. It is a truthful and beautiful work. . . . No one can read it without feeling strengthened and purified."—*Globe.*

"We can be sincere in our praise of this book: we have been often touched by the tone of loving sympathy in which it is written."—*Examiner.*

"This work cannot fail to be of the deepest interest; and it has a special interest for female readers."—*Economist.*

"The whole strange and pathetic story of the Brontë family is faithfully told in Mrs. Gaskell's memoir."—*Critic.*

VIII.

The Militiaman at Home and Abroad;
Being the History of a Militia Regiment.
With Illustrations, by JOHN LEECH. Post 8vo. 9s. cloth.

"The author is humorous without being wilfully smart, sarcastic without bitterness, and shrewd without parading his knowledge and power of observation."—*Express.*

"We have before us the remarks and observations of an intelligent man."—*Economist.*

"Very amusing, and conveying an impression of faithfulness."—*National Review.*

IX.

Antiquities of Kertch, and Researches in the Cimmerian Bosphorus. By DUNCAN McPHERSON, M.D., of the Madras Army, F.R.G.S., M.A.I., Inspector - General of Hospitals, Turkish Contingent.

Imperial Quarto, with Fourteen Plates and numerous Illustrations, including Eight Coloured Fac-Similes of Relics of Antique Art, price Two Guineas.

"It is a volume which deserves the careful attention of every student of classical antiquity. No one can fail to be pleased with a volume which has so much to attract the eye and to gratify the love of beauty and elegance in design. . . . . The volume is got up with great care and taste, and forms one of the handsomest works that have recently issued from the English Press."—*Saturday Review.*

NEW PUBLICATIONS—*continued.*

x.

The Life and Correspondence of Sir John Malcolm, *G.C.B.* By JOHN WILLIAM KAYE.

Two Volumes, 8vo. With Portrait. Price 36s. cloth.

"The biography is replete with interest and information, deserving to be perused by the student of Indian history, and sure to recommend itself to the general reader."—*Athenæum.*

"One of the most interesting of the recent biographies of our great Indian statesmen."—*National Review.*

"This book deserves to participate in the popularity which it was the good fortune of Sir John Malcolm to enjoy."—*Edinburgh Review.*

"Mr. Kaye has used his materials well, and has written an interesting narrative, copiously illustrated with valuable documents."—*Examiner.*

xi.

Life and Sermons of Tauler. Translated from the German, with Notices of Tauler's Life and Times. By MISS SUSANNA WINKWORTH. And a Preface by the REV. CHARLES KINGSLEY.

Small 4to, Printed on Tinted Paper, and bound in antique style, with red edges, suitable for a Present. Price 15s.

"No difference of opinion can be felt as to the intrinsic value of these sermons, or the general interest attaching to this book."—*Athenæum.*

"Miss Winkworth has done a service not only to church history and to literature, but

to those who seek simple and true-hearted devotional reading, by producing a deeply-interesting life of Tauler, and giving us his sermons, tastefully and vigorously translated."—*Guardian.*

xii.

Third Series of Sermons. By the late REV. FRED. W. ROBERTSON, A.M., Incumbent of Trinity Chapel, Brighton.

Post 8vo, with Portrait, price 9s. cloth.

FIRST SERIES—*Third Edition, Post 8vo, price 9s. cloth.*

SECOND SERIES—*Third Edition, price 9s. cloth.*

"Very beautiful in feeling and occasionally striking and forcible in conception to a remarkable degree."—*Guardian.*

"Mr. Robertson, of Brighton, is a name familiar to most of us, and honoured by all to whom it is familiar. A true servant of Christ, a bold and heart-stirring preacher of the Gospel, his teaching was beautified and intensified by genius. New truth, new light, streamed from each well-worn text when he

handled it. The present volume is rich in evidence of his pious, manly, and soaring faith, and of his power not only to point to heaven, but to lead the way."—*Globe.*

"These sermons are full of thought and beauty. There is not a sermon in the series that does not furnish evidence of originality without extravagance, of discrimination without tediousness, and of piety without cant or conventionalism."—*British Quarterly.*

xiii.

A Visit to Salt Lake; Being a Journey across the Plains to the Mormon Settlements at Utah. By WILLIAM CHANDLESS.

Post 8vo, with a Map, price 9s. cloth.

"At length we have an English writer who has been to Salt Lake, and tells us all about it: he pledges his word to the accuracy of every conversation and every incident in his

book. It has impressed us with the conviction that this strange heresy and schism of the nineteenth century has a stronger vitality than we had previously dreamt."—*Athenæum.*

xiv.

Hand-Book of British Maritime Law. By D. R. MORICE, Advocate.

8vo, Price 5s., cloth.

WORKS OF MR. RUSKIN.

I.

The Elements of Drawing. By JOHN RUSKIN, M.A.

Crown 8vo. With Illustrations drawn by the Author. Price 7s. 6d. cloth.

"The rules are clearly and fully laid down; and the earlier exercises always conducive to the end by simple and unembarrassing means. . . . . To be entertaining is a great gift in a writer. This gift Mr. Ruskin possesses pre-eminently. The whole volume is full of liveliness."—*Spectator.*

"We close this book with a feeling that, though nothing supersedes a master, yet that no student of art should launch forth without this work as a compass."—*Athenæum.*

"It will be found not only an invaluable acquisition to the student, but agreeable and instructive reading for any one who wishes to refine his perceptions of natural scenery, and of its worthiest artistic representations."—*Economist.*

"The rules and illustrations will be found to be unusually concise, pertinent, and available . . . . Original as this treatise is, it cannot fail to be at once instructive and suggestive."—*Literary Gazette.*

"The most useful and practical book on the subject which has ever come under our notice."—*Press.*

II.

Notes on the Principal Pictures at the Royal Academy, &c. No. III., 1857.

Second Edition, with Postscript. 8vo, price One Shilling.

III.

Notes on the Turner Collection.

Fifth Edition, Revised, with Preface, 8vo, price One Shilling.

IV.

Pre-Raphaelitism.

8vo, 2s. sewed.

"We wish that this pamphlet might be largely read by our art-patrons, and studied by our art-critics. There is much to be collected from it which is very important to remember."—*Guardian.*

V.

Modern Painters, Vol. IV. On Mountain Beauty.

Imperial 8vo, with Thirty-five Illustrations engraved on Steel, and 116 Woodcuts, drawn by the Author, price 2l. 10s. cloth.

"Considered as an illustrated volume, this is the most remarkable which Mr. Ruskin has yet issued. The plates and woodcuts are profuse, and include numerous drawings of mountain form by the author, which prove Mr. Ruskin to be essentially an artist. Keen sight, keen feeling, and keen power of expression are the qualities which go to the making of an artist, and all these Mr. Ruskin possesses. He adds to them a peculiarly subtle turn for theory, investigation and exposition. This combination makes him an unique man, both among artists and writers."—*Spectator.*

"The present volume of Mr. Ruskin's elaborate work treats chiefly of mountain scenery, and discusses at length the principles involved in the pleasure we derive from mountains and their pictorial representation. The author is more philosophical and less critical than before. Mr. Ruskin occupies a peculiar position as a writer. He compels his most vehement adversaries to admire even while they dissent. The singular beauty of his style, the hearty sympathy with all forms of natural loveliness, the profusion of his illustrations, and above all the earnest denunciation of cant, form irresistible attractions. You may quarrel with the critic, but you cannot fail to admire the writer and respect the man. High thoughts, clothed in eloquent language, are the characteristics of Mr. Ruskin's productions."—*Daily News.*

WORKS OF MR. RUSKIN—*continued.*

VI.

Modern Painters, Vol. III. *Of Many Things.*

With Eighteen Illustrations drawn by the Author, and engraved on Steel,
price 38s. cloth.

" This book may be taken up with equal pleasure whether the reader be acquainted or not with the previous volumes, and no special artistic culture is necessary in order to enjoy its excellences or profit by its suggestions. Every one who cares about nature, or poetry, or the story of human development—every one who has a tinge of literature or philosophy, will find something that is for him in this volume."—*Westminster Review.*

" Mr. Ruskin's third volume of 'Modern Painters' will be hailed with interest and curiosity, if not with submissive attention, by the Art-world of England. . . . . Mr. Ruskin is in possession of a clear and penetrating mind ; he is undeniably practical in his fundamental ideas; full of the deepest reverence for all that appears to him beautiful and holy, and, though owing to very strong preferences, founding those preferences on reason. . . . . His style is, as usual, clear, bold, and racy. Mr. Ruskin is one of the first writers of the day."—*Economist.*

" The present volume, viewed as a literary achievement, is the highest and most striking evidence of the author's abilities that has yet been published. It shows the maturity of his powers of thought, and the perfection of his grace of style."—*Leader.*

" All, it is to be hoped, will read the book for themselves. They will find it well worth a careful perusal. This third volume fully realizes the expectations we had formed of it."—*Saturday Review.*

VII.

Modern Painters.

Imperial 8vo. Vol. I. Fifth Edition, 18s. cloth.
Vol. II. Fourth Edition, 10s. 6d. cloth.

" Mr. Ruskin's work will send the painter more than ever to the study of nature ; will train men who have always been delighted spectators of nature, to be also attentive observers. Our critics will learn to admire, and mere admirers will learn how to criticise : thus a public will be educated."—*Blackwood's Magazine.*

" A generous and impassioned review of the works of living painters. A hearty and earnest work, full of deep thought, and developing great and striking truths in art."—*British Quarterly Review.*

" A very extraordinary and delightful book, full of truth and goodness, of power and beauty."—*North British Review.*

VIII.

The Stones of Venice.

New complete in Three Volumes, Imperial 8vo, with Fifty-three Plates and numerous Woodcuts, drawn by the Author. Price 5l. 15s. 6d., in embossed cloth, with top edge gilt.

EACH VOLUME MAY BE HAD SEPARATELY.

Vol. I. THE FOUNDATIONS, *with 21 Plates, price 2l. 2s.*
Vol. II. THE SEA STORIES, *with 20 Plates, price 2l. 2s.*
Vol. III. THE FALL, *with 12 Plates, price 1l. 11s. 6d.*

" This book is one which, perhaps, no other man could have written, and one for which the world ought to be and will be thankful. It is in the highest degree eloquent, acute, stimulating to thought, and fertile in suggestion. It shows a power of practical criticism which, when fixed on a definite object, nothing absurd or evil can withstand ; and a power of appreciation which has restored treasures of beauty to mankind. It will, we are convinced, elevate taste and intellect, raise the tone of moral feeling, kindle benevolence towards men, and increase the love and fear of God."—*Times.*

" The 'Stones of Venice' is the production of an earnest, religious, progressive, and intellectual architecture has condensed into it a poetic apprehension, the fruit of awe of God, and delight in nature ; a knowledge, love, and just estimate of art ; a holding fast to fact and repudiation of hearsay; an historic breadth, and a fearless challenge of existing social problems, whose union we know not where to find paralleled."—*Spectator.*

" No one who has visited Venice can read this book without having a richer glow thrown over his remembrances of that city, and for those who have not, Mr. Ruskin paints it with a firmness of outline and vividness of colouring that will bring it before the imagination with the force of reality."—*Literary Gazette.*

WORKS OF MR. RUSKIN—*continued.*

IX.

The Seven Lamps of Architecture.

Second Edition, with Fourteen Plates drawn by the Author. Imperial 8vo, price 1l. 1s. cloth.

" By the ' Seven Lamps of Architecture,' we understand Mr. Ruskin to mean the seven fundamental and cardinal laws, the observance of and obedience to which are indispensable to the architect, who would deserve the name. The politician, the moralist, the divine, will find in it ample store of instructive matter, as well as the artist. The author of this work belongs to a class of thinkers of whom we have too few among us."—*Examiner.*

" Mr. Ruskin's book bears so unmistakeably the marks of keen and accurate observation, of a true and subtle judgment and refined sense of beauty, joined with so much earnestness, so noble a sense of the purposes and business of art, and such a command of rich and glowing language, that it cannot but tell powerfully in producing a more religious view of the uses of architecture, and a deeper insight into its artistic principles."—*Guardian.*

X.

Lectures on Architecture and Painting.

With Fourteen Cuts drawn by the Author. Second Edition. Crown 8vo, price 8s. 6d. cloth.

" Mr. Ruskin's Lectures—eloquent, graphic, and impassioned—exposing and ridiculing some of the vices of our present system of building, and exciting his hearers by strong motives of duty and pleasure to attend to architecture—are very successful; and, like his former works, will command public attention. His style is terse, vigorous, and sparkling, and his book is both animated and attractive."—*Economist.*

" We conceive it to be impossible that any

intelligent persons could listen to the lectures, however they might differ from the judgments asserted, and from the general propositions laid down, without an elevating influence and an aroused enthusiasm, which are often more fruitful in producing true taste and correct views of art than the soundest historical generalizations and the most learned technical criticism in which the heart and the senses own no interest."—*Spectator.*

XI.

The Opening of the Crystal Palace;

Considered in some of its relations to the Prospects of Art.
8vo, price 1s. sewed.

" An earnest and eloquent appeal for the preservation of the ancient monuments of Gothic architecture."—*English Churchman.*

" A wholesome and much needed protest."—*Leader.*

XII.

The King of the Golden River; or, the Black Brothers.

Third Edition, with 22 Illustrations by RICHARD DOYLE. *Price 2s. 6d.*

" This little fairy tale is by a master hand. The story has a charming moral, and the writing is so excellent, that it would be hard

to say which it will give most pleasure to, the very wise man or the very simple child."—*Examiner.*

XIII.

Examples of the Architecture of Venice,

Selected and Drawn to Measurement from the Edifices.

In Parts of Folio Imperial size, each containing Five Plates, and a short Explanatory Text, price 1l. 1s. each.

PARTS I. TO III. ARE PUBLISHED.

Fifty India Proofs only are taken on Atlas Folio, price 2l. 2s. each Part.

RECENT WORKS.

Annals of British Legislation, a *Classified Summary of Parliamentary Papers.* Edited by Professor LEONE LEVI. The Yearly Issue will consist of 1000 pages super royal 8vo, the subscription for which is Two Guineas, payable in advance. The successive parts will be delivered post free, and to subscribers only.

THE SIXTEENTH PART IS JUST ISSUED.

"A series that, if it be always managed as it is now by Professor Levi, will last as long as there remains a legislature in Great Britain."—*Examiner.*

"Such a work is much needed."—*Economist.*

"It would not be easy to over-estimate the utility of Professor Levi's serial. It has the merit of being an excellent idea zealously carried out."—*Athenæum.*

"We cannot imagine a more truly valuable and nationally important work than this. It is impossible to over-estimate its usefulness."—*Civil Service Gazette.*

A Residence in Tasmania. By CAPTAIN H. BUTLER STONEY.

Demy 8vo, with Plates, Cuts, and a Map, price 14s. cloth.

"A perfect guide-book to Van Diemen's Land, describing simply and faithfully the country, the plants, animals, and people in it."—*Examiner.*

"A plain and clear account of the colonies in Van Diemen's Land, which besides being very agreeable reading may be confidently consulted on all matters connected with their material resources, actual position, and social industrial aspects."—*Athenæum.*

Sight-Seeing in Germany and the Tyrol, in the Autumn of 1855. By SIR JOHN FORBES, Author of "A Physician's Holiday," &c.

Post 8vo, with Map and View, price 10s. 6d. cloth.

"The ground is described clearly, the things that appeared most worth seeing to a sensible, observant tourist, are set down, together with the natural impressions they produced, and the result is a work more agreeable in every way than many a book of travel."—*Examiner.*

The Treatment of the Insane, Without *Mechanical Restraints.* By JOHN CONOLLY, M.D.

Demy 8vo, price 14s. cloth.

"There is not a page which will not be perused with interest, even by a non-professional reader."—*Morning Post.*

A Handbook of Average, for the Use of *Merchants, Shipowners, &c., with a Chapter on Arbitration.* By MANLEY HOPKINS.

8vo, price 12s. 6d. cloth.

Papers of the late Lord Metcalfe. Selected and Edited by J. W. KAYE.

Demy 8vo, price 16s. cloth.

RECENT WORKS—*continued.*

The Political Life of Sir R. Peel.

By THOMAS · DOUBLEDAY, Author of the "Financial History of England," "The True Law of Population," &c.

Two Volumes, Crown 8vo, price 18s. cloth.

"Let all readers, before they take in hand the personal memoirs of Sir Robert Peel, peruse these volumes of Mr. Doubleday: in them the statesman's character and public acts are analysed in the spirit neither of a detractor nor of a panegyrist. This biography is a work of great merit, conscientiously prepared, plain, clear, and practically interesting."—*Leader.*

The European Revolutions of 1848.

By EDWARD CAYLEY.

Two Volumes, Crown 8vo, price 18s. cloth.

"Mr. Cayley has produced a book which is in many respects good, which might have been better, but which, so far from having been yet superseded, has not at present even a competitor. As far as our examination has gone, we have found it generally accurate; and independently of its accuracy it is valuable for two qualities—the sturdy common sense and pleasant humour of the author. It is also in the main practical and sound."—*Times.*

Signs of the Times: or, *The Dangers to Religious Liberty in the Present Day.* By the CHEVALIER BUNSEN. Translated by Miss SUSANNA WINKWORTH.

One Volume, 8vo, price 16s. cloth.

"An investigation of the religious principles at work in the Christian world; tracing, as far as modern politics extend, the action of priesthood, associations, and secular decrees enforcing spiritual dogmas. It is the most remarkable work that has appeared in modern times from the pen of a statesman."—*Leader.*

The History, Topography, and Antiquities of the Isle of Wight. By DAVENPORT ADAMS.

Quarto, 25 Steel Plates, cloth, gilt edges, price 2l. 2s.

Stories and Sketches. By JAMES PAYN.

Post 8vo, Price 8s. 6d. cloth.

"Mr. Payn is gay, spirited, observant; and shows no little knowledge of men and books."—*Leader.*

"A volume of pleasant reading."—*Literary Gazette.*

Round the Fire: Six *Stories for Young Readers.* By the Author of "The Day of a Baby Boy."

Square 16mo, with Frontispiece, price 3s. cloth.

"These stories are supposed to be told by six little girls. The language is child-like and winning, and makes us feel that we are reading true children's stories."—*Athenæum.*

RECENT WORKS—*continued.*

Rifle Practice. By LIEUTENANT-COLONEL JOHN JACOB, C.B.
With Plates. Third Edition, revised and enlarged, price 2s.

Two Summer Cruises with the Baltic
Fleet in 1854-5; *Being the Log of the " Pet."* By R. E. HUGHES, M.A.
Second Edition, Post 8vo, with Views and Charts. 10s. 6d., cloth.

The Court of Henry VIII.: Being a
Selection of the Despatches of SEBASTIAN GIUSTINIAN, Venetian Ambassador, 1515-1519. Translated by RAWDON BROWN.
Two Vols., crown 8vo, price 21s. cloth.

A Campaign with the Turks in Asia.
By CHARLES DUNCAN.
Two Vols., post 8vo, price 21s. cloth.

The Red River Settlement. By
ALEXANDER ROSS, Author of "Fur Hunters in the Far West."
One Volume, post 8vo, price 10s. 6d. cloth.

The Fur-Hunters of the Far West.
By ALEXANDER ROSS.
Two Volumes, post 8vo. With Map and Plate. 21s. cloth.

Russo-Turkish Campaigns of 1828-9.
By COLONEL CHESNEY, R.A., D.C.L., F.R.S.
Third Edition. Post 8vo, with Maps, price 12s. cloth.

Military Forces and Institutions of
Great Britain. By H. BYERLEY THOMSON, of the Inner Temple.
8vo, 15s. cloth.

A Manual of the Mercantile Law of
Great Britain and Ireland. By PROFESSOR LEONE LEVI, Author of "Commercial Law of the World."
8vo, price 12s. cloth.

The Laws of War Affecting Commerce and Shpping. By H. BYERLEY THOMSON, of the Inner Temple.
Second Edition, greatly enlarged. 8vo, price 4s. 6d. boards.

CHEAP EDITION OF THE WORKS OF CURRER BELL.

Jane Eyre.   By CURRER BELL.

New Edition. Small Post 8vo, price 2s. 6d. cloth.

"'Jane Eyre' is a remarkable production. Freshness and originality, truth and passion, singular felicity in the description of natural scenery, and in the analysation of human thought, enable this tale to stand boldly out from the mass, and to assume its own place in the bright field of romantic literature."—*Times.*

Shirley.   By CURRER BELL.

New Edition. Small Post 8vo, price 2s. 6d. cloth.   (Just ready.)

"The peculiar power which was so greatly admired in 'Jane Eyre' is not absent from this book. It possesses deep interest, and an irresistible grasp of reality. There are scenes which, for strength and delicacy of emotion, are not transcended in the range of English fiction."—*Examiner.*

Villette.   By CURRER BELL.

New Edition. Small Post 8vo, price 2s. 6d. cloth.   (Nearly ready.)

"This novel amply sustains the fame of the author of 'Jane Eyre' and 'Shirley' as an original and powerful writer."—*Examiner.*

Wuthering Heights.   By ELLIS BELL.

Agnes Grey.   By ACTON BELL.

(In the Press.)

WORKS OF MR. THACKERAY.

Lectures on the English Humourists

of the 18th Century.   By W. M. THACKERAY, Author of "Vanity Fair," "The Newcomes," &c.

Second Edition. Crown 8vo, price 10s. 6d. cloth.

"To those who attended the lectures, the book will be a pleasant reminiscence, to others an exciting novelty. The style—clear, idiomatic, forcible, familiar, but never slovenly; the searching strokes of sarcasm or irony; the occasional flashes of generous scorn; the touches of pathos, pity, and tenderness; the morality tempered but never weakened by experience and sympathy; the felicitous phrases, the striking anecdotes, the passages of wise, practical reflection; all these lose much less than we could have expected from the absence of the voice, manner, and look of the lecturer."—*Spectator.*

Esmond.   By W. M. THACKERAY.

Second Edition. 3 vols., Crown 8vo, reduced to 15s. cloth.

"Mr. Thackeray has selected for his hero a very noble type of the cavalier softening into the man of the eighteenth century, and for his heroine one of the sweetest women that ever breathed from canvas or from book, since Raffaelle painted and Shakspeare wrote. The style is manly, clear, terse, and vigorous, reflecting every mood—pathetic, graphic, or sarcastic—of the writer."—*Spectator.*

The Rose and the Ring; or the

History of Prince Giglio and Prince Bulbo.   By MR. M. A. TITMARSH.

With 58 Cuts drawn by the Author.   3rd Edition, price 5s.

NEW NOVELS.

Farina: a *Legend of Cologne.* By GEORGE MEREDITH, Author of "The Shaving of Shagpät." 1 vol.   *Post 8vo, 10s. 6d. cloth.*

Lucian Playfair. By THOMAS MACKERN. 3 vols.

The Professor. By CURRER BELL, Author of "Jane Eyre," "Shirley," "Villette," &c.   2 vols.

"We think the friends of Charlotte Brontë have shown sound judgment in publishing 'The Professor.' It throws a strong light on many of the characteristic turns of her thought, on her most cherished feelings, and on the position she assumed towards her neighbours and acquaintances. It opens a new chapter in the curious psychological study afforded by the history of this generous, passionate recluse. It shows the first germs of conception, which afterwards expanded and ripened into the great creations of her imagination." — *Saturday Review.*

"We have read it with the deepest interest, and confidently predict that this legacy of Charlotte Brontë's genius will renew and confirm the general admiration of her extraordinary powers."—*Eclectic Review.*

"The idea is original, and we every here and there detect germs of that power which took the world by storm in 'Jane Eyre.' The rejection of the 'Professor' was, in our opinion, no less advantageous to the young authoress than creditable to the discernment of the booksellers."—*Press.*

"For the novelist 'The Professor' will be an interesting study."—*Globe.*

Below the Surface: a *Story of English Country Life.* 3 vols.

"The book is unquestionably clever and entertaining. It is a tale superior to ordinary novels in its practical application to the phases of actual life."—*Athenæum.*

"It is a novel worth reading, and some parts of it are worth remembering. The story offers many points of interest and dramatic power; and there is considerable humour in some of the scenes."—*Economist.*

"The novel keeps the attention fixed, and it is written in a genial, often playful tone. The temper is throughout excellent."—*Examiner.*

The Roua Pass; or, *Englishmen in the Highlands.* By ERICK MACKENZIE. 3 vols.

The Eve of St. Mark: a *Romance of Venice.* By THOMAS DOUBLEDAY. 2 vols.

Friends of Bohemia; or, *Phases of London Life.* By E. M. WHITTY, Author of "The Governing Classes." 2 vols., post 8vo.

Oliver Cromwell: a *Story of the Civil Wars.* By CHAS. EDWARD STEWART. 2 vols.

Florence Templar. 1 vol.

Kathie Brande: *The Fireside History of a Quiet Life.* By HOLME LEE, Author of "Gilbert Massenger," "Thorney Hall," &c. 2 vols.

NOVELS FORTHCOMING.

Riverston. By GEORGIANA M. CRAIK. 3 vols.
(Just ready.)

The Moors and the Fens. By F. G. TRAFFORD. 3 vols.

Gaston Bligh. By L. S. LAVENU, Author of " Erlesmere." 2 vols.

The Noble Traytour. *A Chronicle.* 3 vols.

The Three Chances. By the Author of " The Fair Carew." 3 vols.

The White House by the Sea. 1 vol.

The Cruelest Wrong. 1 vol.

RECENT NOVELS.

Tender and True. By the Author of " Clara Morison." 2 vols.

Young Singleton. By TALBOT GWYNNE, Author of " The School for Fathers," &c. 2 vols.

Erlesmere. By L. S. LAVENU. 2 vols.

Perversion: or, *The Causes and Consequences of Infidelity.* Second Edition. 3 vols.

Beyminstre. By the Author of " Lena." 3 vols.

After Dark. By WILKIE COLLINS. 2 vols.

Amberhill. By A. J. BARROWCLIFFE. 2 vols.

Leonora. By the Hon. MRS. MABERLY. 3 vols.

Eveleen. By E. L. A. BERWICK. 3 vols.

Maurice Elvington. By WILFRID EAST. 3 vols.

ORIENTAL.

The Chinese and their Rebellions.
By THOMAS TAYLOR MEADOWS.
One Thick Volume, 8vo, with Maps, price 18s. cloth.

"Mr. Meadows appears to know China more thoroughly and comprehensively than any of his predecessors. His book is the work of a learned, conscientious, and observant person, and really important in many respects. It is the most curious book we have met with for a long time."—*Times.*

"In this book is a vast amount of valuable information respecting China, and the statements it contains bear on them the face of truth. Mr. Meadows has produced a work which deserves to be studied by all who would gain a true appreciation of Chinese character. Information is sown broad-cast through every page."—*Athenæum.*

Life in Ancient India. By Mrs. SPEIR.
With Sixty Illustrations by G. Scharf. 8vo, price 15s., elegantly bound in cloth, gilt edges.

"We should in vain seek for any other treatise which, in so short a space, gives so well-connected an account of the early period of Indian history."—*Daily News.*

"Whoever desires to have the best, the completest, and the most popular view of what Oriental scholars have made known to us respecting Ancient India must peruse the work of Mrs. Speir; in which he will find the story told in clear, correct, and unaffected English. The book is admirably got up."—*Examiner.*

The Cauvery, Kistnah, and Godavery:
Being a Report on the Works constructed on those Rivers for the Irrigation of Provinces in the Presidency of Madras.
By R. BAIRD SMITH, F.G.S., Lt.-Col. Bengal Engineers, &c., &c.
In demy 8vo, with 19 Plans, price 28s. cloth.

"A most curious and interesting work."—*Economist.*

The Bhilsa Topes; or, Buddhist Monuments of
Central India. By Major CUNNINGHAM.
One Volume, 8vo, with Thirty-three Plates, price 30s. cloth.

"Of the Topes opened in various parts of India none have yielded so rich a harvest of important information as those of Bhilsa, opened by Major Cunningham and Lieut. Maisey; and which are described, with an abundance of highly curious graphic illustrations, in this most interesting book."—*Examiner.*

Travels and Adventures in Assam.
By Major JOHN BUTLER.
One Volume 8vo, with Plates, price 12s. cloth.

"This volume is unusually successful in creating an interest on an Eastern subject. It is illustrated by views of landscapes, figures, and antiquities."—*Press.*

The English in Western India; Being
the Early History of the Factory at Surat, of Bombay.
By PHILIP ANDERSON, A.M.
Second Edition, 8vo, price 14s. cloth.

"Quaint, curious, and amusing, this volume describes, from old manuscripts and obscure books, the life of English merchants in an Indian Factory. It contains fresh and amusing gossip, all bearing on events and characters of historical importance."—*Athenæum.*

"A book of permanent value."—*Guardian.*

ORIENTAL—*continued.*

Dr. Royle on the Fibrous Plants of India Fitted for Cordage, Clothing, and Paper. 8vo, price 12s. cloth.

Dr. Royle on the Culture and Commerce of Cotton in India. 8vo, 18s. cloth.

Dr. Wilson on Infanticide in Western India. Demy 8vo, price 12s.

Rev. James Coley's Journal of the Sutlej Campaign. Fcap. 8vo, price 5s. cloth.

Crawfurd's Grammar and Dictionary of the Malay Language. 2 vols. 8vo, price 36s. cloth.

Roberts's Indian Exchange Tables. 8vo. Second Edition, enlarged, price 10s. 6d. cloth.

Waring on Abscess in the Liver. 8vo, price 3s. 6d.

Laurie's Pegu. Post 8vo, price 14s. cloth.

Boyd's Turkish Interpreter: a Grammar of the Turkish Language. 8vo, price 12s.

Bridgnell's Indian Commercial Tables. Royal 8vo, price 21s., half-bound.

The Bombay Quarterly Review. Nos. 1 to 8, price 5s. each.

Baillie's Land Tax of India. According to the Moohummudan Law. 8vo, price 6s. cloth.

Baillie's Moohummudan Law of Sale. 8vo, price 14s. cloth.

Irving's Theory and Practice of Caste. 8vo, price 5s. cloth.

Gingell's Ceremonial Usages of the Chinese. Imperial 8vo, price 9s. cloth.

The Insurrection in China. By Dr. YVAN and M. CALLERY. Translated by JOHN OXENFORD. Third Edition. Post 8vo, with Chinese Map and Portrait, price 7s. 6d. cloth.

Kesson's Cross and the Dragon; or, The Fortunes of Christianity in China. Post 8vo, 6s. cloth.

MISCELLANEOUS.

Elementary Works on Social Economy. Uniform in foolscap 8vo, half-bound.

    I.—OUTLINES OF SOCIAL ECONOMY. 1*s*. 6*d*.
    II.—PROGRESSIVE LESSONS IN SOCIAL SCIENCE. 1*s*. 6*d*.
    III.—INTRODUCTION TO THE SOCIAL SCIENCES. 2*s*.
    IV.—QUESTIONS AND ANSWERS ON THE ARRANGEMENTS AND RELATIONS OF SOCIAL LIFE. 2*s*. 6*d*.
    V.—OUTLINES OF THE UNDERSTANDING. 2*s*.
    VI.—WHAT AM I? WHERE AM I? WHAT OUGHT I TO DO? &c. 1*s*. sewed.

Swainson's Lectures on New Zealand. Crown 8vo, price 2*s*. 6*d*. cloth.

Swainson's Account of Auckland. Post 8vo, with a view, price 6*s*. cloth.

Playford's Hints for Investing Money. Second Edition, post 8vo, price 2*s*. 6*d*. cloth.

Sir John Forbes's Memorandums in Ireland. Two Vols., post 8vo, price 1*l*. 1*s*. cloth.

Leigh Hunt's Men, Women, and Books. Two Vols., price 10*s*. cloth.

    ———— *Table Talk.* 3*s*. 6*d*. cloth.
    ———— *Wit and Humour.* 5*s*. cloth.
    ———— *Imagination and Fancy.* 5*s*. cloth.
    ———— *Jar of Honey.* 5*s*. cloth.

Sir John Herschel's Astronomical Observations made at the Cape of Good Hope. 4to, with plates, price 4*l*. 4*s*. cloth.

Darwin's Geological Observations on Coral Reefs, Volcanic Islands, and on South America. With maps, plates, and woodcuts, 10*s*. 6*d*. cloth.

Levi's Commercial Law of the World. Two Vols., royal 4to, price 6*l*. cloth.

Juvenile Delinquency. By M. HILL and C. F. CORNWALLIS. Post 8vo, price 6*s*. cloth.

Doubleday's True Law of Population. Third Edition, 8vo, 10*s*. cloth.

McCann's Argentine Provinces, &c. Two Vols., post 8vo, with illustrations, price 24*s*. cloth.

Rowcroft's Tales of the Colonies. Fifth Edition. 6*s*. cloth.

Goethe's Conversations with Eckermann. Translated by JOHN OXENFORD. Two Vols., post 8vo, 10*s*. cloth.

Kavanagh's Women of Christianity Exemplary for Piety and Charity. Post 8vo, with Portraits, price 12*s*., in embossed cloth, gilt edges.

POETRY.

England in Time of War. By SYDNEY DOBELL, Author of "Balder," "The Roman," &c.   Crown 8vo, 5s. cloth.

" 'England in Time of War' is a series of lyrics representing the emotions of those who are left at home to bear the passive sorrows of war, and of those who go out to brave its perils."—*Westminster Review.*

"That Mr. Dobell is a poet, 'England in time of War' bears witness in many single lines, and in two or three short poems."—*Athenæum.*

The Cruel Sister, AND OTHER POEMS.   Fcap. 8vo, 4s. cloth.

Poems of Past Years. By Sir ARTHUR HALLAM ELTON, Bart., M.P.   Fcap. 8vo, 3s. cloth.

Poems. By Mrs. FRANK P. FELLOWS.   Fcap. 8vo, 3s. cloth.

" There is easy simplicity in the diction, and elegant naturalness in the thought."—*Spectator.*

Lota, AND OTHER POEMS.   By DEVON HARRIS. Fcap. 8vo, 4s. cloth.

"Displaying high poetic genius and power."—*Eclectic Review.*

Poetry from Life. By C. M. K.   Fcap. 8vo, cloth gilt, 5s.

" Elegant verses.   The author has a pleasing fancy and a refined mind."—*Economist.*

" In some of the pieces of this genial and pleasant volume we are reminded of good old George Herbert."—*Literary Gazette.*

Poems. By WALTER R. CASSELS.   Fcap. 8vo, price 3s. 6d. cloth.

" Mr. Cassels has deep poetical feeling, and gives promise of real excellence.   His poems are written sometimes with a strength of expression by no means common.   In quiet narrative and the description of a particular state of feeling, and the presentation of a single thought or image, he shows great power."—*Guardian.*

Garlands of Verse. By THOMAS LEIGH.   Fcap. 8vo, 5s. cloth.

" One of the best things in the 'Garlands of Verse' is an Ode to Toil.   There, as elsewhere, there is excellent feeling."—*Examiner.*

Balder. By SYDNEY DOBELL.   Crown 8vo, 7s. 6d. cloth.

" The writer has fine qualities; his level of thought is lofty, and his passion for the beautiful has the truth of instinct."—*Athenæum.*

Poems. By WILLIAM BELL SCOTT.   Fcap. 8vo, with Three Etchings, price 5s. cloth.

"Mr. Scott has poetical feeling, keen observation, deep thought, and command of language."—*Spectator.*

Poems. By MARY MAYNARD.   Fcap. 8vo, 4s. cloth.

" We have rarely met with a volume of poems displaying so large an amount of power, blended with so much delicacy of feeling and grace of expression."—*Church of England Quarterly.*

Poems. By CURRER, ELLIS, and ACTON BELL.   Fcap. 8vo, 4s. cloth.

Select Odes of Horace. In English Lyrics.   By J. T. BLACK.   Fcap. 8vo, price 4s. cloth.

London: Printed by SMITH, ELDER & Co., Little Green Arbour Court.

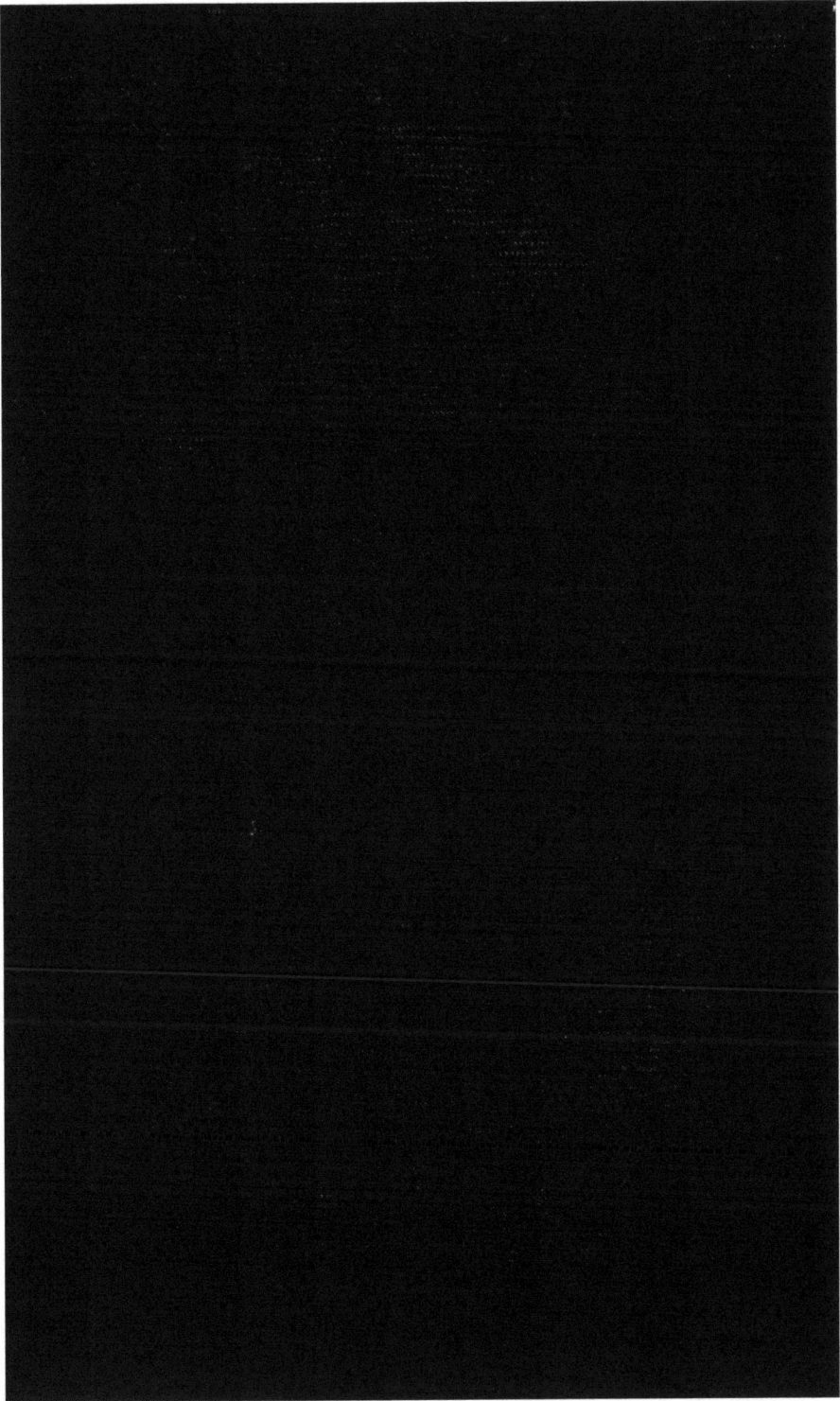

Lightning Source UK Ltd.
Milton Keynes UK
UKHW030839020622
403888UK00007B/839